# Living In The Country

## An Owner's Manual

**Finnlee P. Walter**

FVR Publishing

Cover Design by Finnlee P. Walter
Illustrations by Finnlee P. Walter


For additional information please contact FVR Publishing at 144 Four Notch Rd. Huntsville, Texas 77340

ISBN-13: 979-8-218-33530-4

# Dedication

To Daisygrace, my old girl.
*Forever in my heart.*

# Contents

## Section 2 - Property Enhancements and Maintenance

## Section 3 - The Logistics of Country Living

# Introduction

# Now What?

Rarely does one purchase a new home or rural property and is so perfectly satisfied with it that they have no desire to make any changes. Everyone wants to make their property in their own style. Everyone has specific ideas, hopes, and thoughts about how they would like to change this or that around their property. If only you knew where to start and how to do these *things*. Now What?

The purpose of this book is to help you learn how to do these tasks. There are many daily tasks that come with owning and maintaining a rural property. This book will give you insight on the best practices and help you along the way.

Whether you own a newly built home on a rural one acre plot, or you just bought a 100 year old home on several hundred acres, the information in this book will help you understand how to do those daily tasks. This book will help you learn how to do *things*.

## *Property Groundworks*

Moving to a new home is always exciting and hectic at first. Moving to a new country homestead presents even more challenges, depending on your particular property. If you just bought a piece of raw land with absolutely no structures, roads, fences, or anything else in place already, then you will have different priorities than someone who just bought a brand new home on a rural ranchette. While the job of building your property the way that you want may be vastly different in scale, the challenges ahead are the same. You will need to set priorities for what specific tasks need to be accomplished first. For example; if you own raw land, then cutting some type of access road into your property will probably be first on your list. Or if you just bought a newly built home, fencing and entrance gates for security may be your priority. Installing an simple electric entrance gate can be easily accomplished with the correct knowledge and guidelines.

Property security is important, and learning how to select and set up security cameras around your property will be helpful. If you need to build a fence next to a neighbor's adjoining property, learn how to approach the subject with your new neighbor and what should you do if you need to build a fence by yourself.

Regardless of which tasks that you wish to complete first, this book will explain the job at hand, and whenever possible, present various options with advantages and disadvantages for each.

## *Maintenance And Enhancements*

Rural property maintenance can be a time consuming and overwhelming chore if not done properly. Prepping for the upcoming seasonal changes can be rushed and frantic if you haven't planned ahead properly. Not understanding how to maintain a water well or septic system can be an expensive mistake. This book will outline the typical daily and seasonal maintenance tasks that you will face.

For example, prepping for a hard winter freeze is best done while it is a warm and sunny day. Learning how your water well actually works will help you when it comes time to replace the pressure switch. You will also need tools for yard and property maintenance. Learning what tools are actually needed at first can be an important consideration.

## *The Logistics Of Country Living*

Working from home may be an immediate issue for you. Learning how to set up a home office in a rural setting can be important. Spotty cell phone reception and Internet access will need to be addressed. Learning how to install a cell phone amplifier may be necessary. What are the advantages and disadvantages of satellite Internet vs. a private ISP?

You will quickly learn that getting rural package deliveries can present problems for those who live behind gates and fences. Likewise, dealing with the logistics of how to accommodate access onto your property for service people will crop up occasionally.

A small kitchen garden may be in your future and you will need to know how to set it up. Eventually you will need to learn to preserve and store your food conveniently and safely.

---

This book will discuss all of these issues and more. Use this book as a reference and browse the appendixes for additional information if needed. You will quickly learn that even the most unknown and formidable challenges can be broken down into manageable chunks and eventually you will be more self sufficient than ever before.

*Finnlee P. Walter*

# Section 1
# Property Groundwork

# Chapter 1

# Fencing

The old saying that good fences make good neighbors has never been more true than for rural property owners. Fencing issues probably cause the majority of arguments and disagreements between rural neighbors more than anything else. If you think about it, peace and solitude is the driving force that causes city dwellers to move to the country. Nothing instantly destroys this paradise quicker than a neighbor that has shoddy or no fences at all and their animals are constantly intruding onto your land. Fences can keep the peace between landowners and give each peace of mind knowing that their land is secured and safe.

Building fences can take a significant amount of time and money, so it is better to plan ahead and build a proper and sturdy fence that will last as long as possible. By using long established methods of construction, you can build a fence that will withstand the tests of time.

# *Before You Build*

**Boundaries** - Rural property lines, unlike their city counterparts, can be awfully vague and hard to physically establish on the ground. Quite often, property boundary descriptions on property deeds will refer to key landmarks, trees, and buildings that have long since disappeared. Some of these descriptions will be over 100 years old and antiquated in their terminology. As the property is sold and resold through many generations, the landowners just blindly follow these descriptions and rarely take the time to try and actually mark their property accurately.

Sometimes, there is the example of a longtime landowner neighbor who has been on their property for a lifetime and they are blind to any but their mental view of their property boundaries, even though their perspective may be grossly inaccurate. All of these issues can create a strain on relationships between rural landowners. The best advice on property boundary issues is to try to avoid them in the first place.

Before buying your dream property, take a look at the legal property description filed in the courthouse and see if the description will be easily translated into a modern day property survey. If the description of a corner of a potential piece of property says something like, " next to the large pine tree and the Jones barnyard," this should cause concern. Said tree and the Jones barnyard have long since disappeared and who really knows where that point on the ground actually is today. Modern property surveyors have amazing tools at their disposal to define a piece of property, but if the original property description is vague from the beginning, then none of that will matter in the end. Avoid potential legal issues and hard feelings with neighbors and try to find property that is easily definable right from the start.

Next is the issue of where on the boundary line to actually build your fence. If an old existing fence is currently right on top of the boundary, then obviously that fence will need to be removed to make way for a new fence. That fence may have been constructed by your neighbor 20 years ago and therefore he "owns" that fence. In a case of boundary fences where neighbors are involved, make sure to come to some sort of agreement before fence construction begins. It actually helps neighbors on both sides of a property boundary when a nice new fence is built. This is a good selling point to your neighbor who may be reluctant to have their fence removed and replaced. Fences are expensive and costs can easily run into thousands of dollars on larger properties. Your elderly farmer neighbor simply may not have enough money on hand to help share construction costs. It can be a delicate situation for sure.

The best course of action is to plan on paying for the entire costs of your new fence by yourself if you are building it, even if the neighbor's cows have been trespassing on your property for years. In the long run, it just makes for much better landowner relationships which is invaluable for many reasons, versus bickering over who will pay to build the new fence. If the neighbors offer to help with labor or even split the cost of materials, then so much the better and you are both off to a great start. If fencing issues with your neighbor just cannot be resolved, you can still build your new fence a foot or so inside your property boundary, and your neighbor's ugly old fence can just remain in place. Just be aware that they will also probably mentally lay claim to that new extra foot of property at some point in the future.

## *Fencing Tools and Supplies*

There is no way to avoid the work involved in construction, but there are tips and tools to make it an easier job. Previous generations of farmers and ranchers have pretty much fine tuned the art of fence building to the point that no effort or materials are wasted. By following their examples you can be assured that your fence will last as long as possible too. Not many tools are needed to build most rural fences. Even though equipment dealers and manufacturers always seem to parade the latest new gimmick to entice you to part with your cash, fences usually can be built with just a few simple tools.

**Hand Tools** - These include fencing pliers, wire stretchers, hand post hole diggers, good leather gloves, and hammers. Fencing pliers can be purchased at most farm stores or feed suppliers and are purpose made for wire fences. They usually have a strong wire cutter and a small hammer surface for driving fence staples into wooden posts. Additionally, they have a small hook to facilitate twisting wire clips used for attaching fence wire to metal T-posts and to facilitate removing driven fence staples.

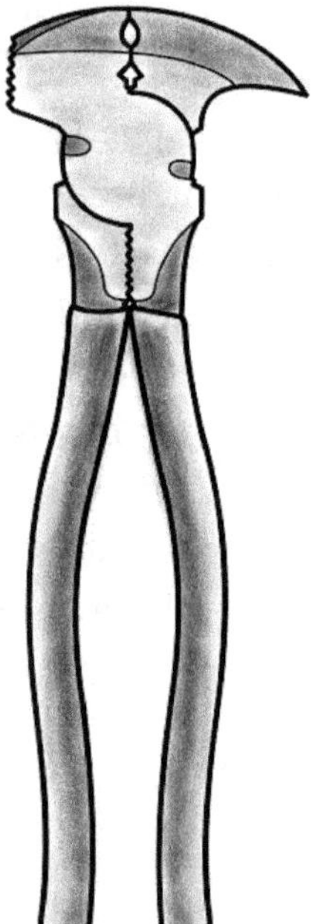

*Fencing Pliers*

Since fencing pliers are usually fairly inexpensive, it can be beneficial to purchase several pairs in advance. This will be handy if several people are working on a fence section at the same time.

Fence wire pullers, or stretchers, are used to stretch a long length of fence wire tight before nailing it to the posts. Barbed wire especially, needs to be very tight for it to be effective against cattle. These stretchers are usually a simple design that grips the wire and braces against a corner post and then pulls the wire tight via a ratcheting handle mechanism. Additionally, these same stretchers can be used to pull together two pieces of broken or damaged fence wire for re-splicing and repair. A good fence stretcher is invaluable to have in your fencing toolkit.

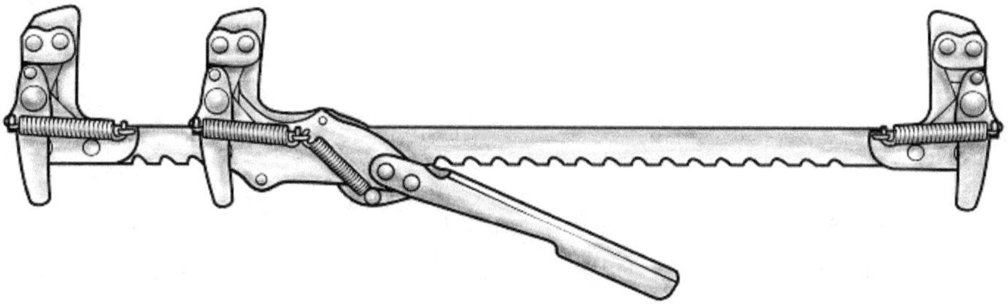

*Fence Wire Stretcher*

For mesh wire or field wire fence designs, a separate puller just for that style of wire may be necessary. These are usually constructed with a wooden bar and wire grips that can then be pulled to tighten the roll of wire mesh evenly without distorting the mesh out of shape. In a pinch, you can substitute a length of common 2x4 lumber for a mesh wire puller. Simply wrap a few turns of the excess end of the wire mesh around the board allowing for even pulling. Using a short length of chain or rope, attach the board to a tractor or a hand winch and slowly pull the wire mesh to the correct tension. After nailing and attaching the mesh to the end posts, the 2x4 board can be removed and the excess mesh wire trimmed away.

If you plan on using metal t-posts in your fencing, then a t-post driver will be necessary. This is usually constructed of a 2 foot length of metal pipe with a welded cap on one end and handles attached to the sides.

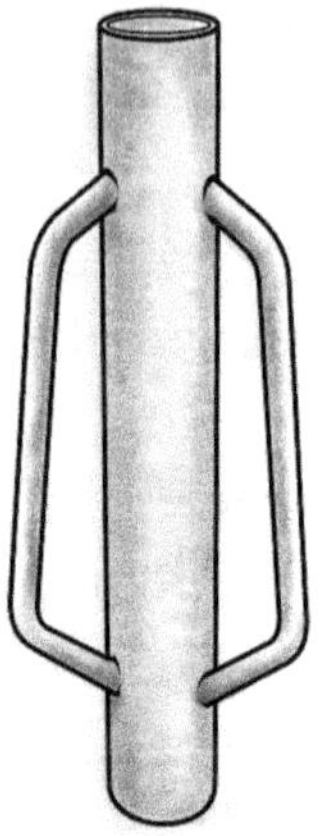

*T-post Driver*

To use a t-post driver, you hold the t-post upright and slide the driver pipe over the top of the post. Then you start raising the driver and hammering down on top of the post. The weight of the driver acts as a sledge hammer of sorts, and drives the t-post into the ground a few inches with each successive blow of the driver. With a bit of practice, you will learn to drive the t-post straight and plumb.

Post hole diggers vary in size and design. Their purpose is to dig a hole just big enough to insert a wooden fence post into the ground. Some are clam shell designs and others look like screw augers with a T-handle. The soil type on your land will dictate which design you will need. If you have rocky soil, a pick axe, and a sturdy metal pry bar will be your tools of choice. Better yet a tractor mounted auger will be the quickest of all of these to use.

A sturdy measuring tape of at least 50 feet in length will be needed to lay out your fence posts evenly along the proposed fence line. Depending on your soil type and general area, wire fence post spacing can range from 8 feet to 15 feet between posts.

Walking along your proposed fence line and marking post locations can be easily and quickly accomplished using a long measuring tape and a can of spray paint to mark each post location on the ground.

Lastly, heavy leather gloves are an absolute necessity for hand protection. The sharp barbs of barbed wire can shred skin and cause painful wounds. Blisters and scrapes and even busted thumbs from hammers can all be avoided by using heavy leather gloves when building fences.

---

**Handy Tip...**
**Paint your fencing hand tools a bright color so that they don't become misplaced and lost in tall grass or weeds while you are building your fence.**

---

**Power Assisted Tools** - If you have a sizable length of fence line to build, a power auger is nearly a necessity. These are defined into two different types. One type is a handheld motor auger that has a small motor attached to handles and the auger. Usually this type of auger takes two people to safely operate. They can make quick work of drilling post holes in soft soil.

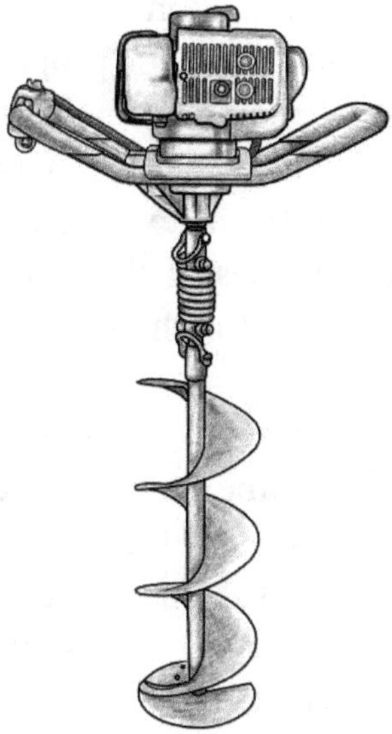

*Motorized Auger*

The other type of power auger attaches to the 3 point lift of a farm tractor and operates via the tractor's engine and PTO shaft attachment. These can be operated by just one person with a bit of practice. There are other types of post drivers that actually pound the fence posts into the ground, but these are usually specialty tools designed for fence building contractors.

## *Types Of Fences*

Most rural fences are built according to a particular need for containment within a defined area. If your fence is intended to hold livestock or other heavy animals, then an appropriately strong fence should be built to contain them in the most adverse conditions. Likewise, if you are just looking at building a general fence along the county road in the front of your property, you probably would like to build a pretty fence that shows off your property to it's best advantage. Cross fencing within the interior of your property, if needed, can be built a bit rougher and cheaper, as it's generally for utility purposes only and not in public view.

The best advice for deciding on what fence style and type to choose is to take a drive around other properties in your immediate area and see what styles of fencing are being used. Many of the older and more established properties in your area probably have multiple fences built through generations of experience. You can leverage this experience and build your fences in the same manner, knowing that what has worked successfully for them will also work successfully for you too.

One last note about fence types, some designs such as steel pipe fencing, vinyl fencing, high game fencing, and tall security chain link fencing, are best installed by a professional fence contractor. These styles require special expertise, manpower, and special tools and equipment to install properly and are usually not practical for the average property owner to tackle.

## *Basic Construction Principles*

Regardless of the type of fence that you plan to build, there are a few common planning and construction steps that pertain to all fences. It is always best to build a long fence in shorter sections. This allows for completion of one section before starting another and will help you learn what additional tools, materials, and construction steps that may be needed, before starting the next section. Every fence seems to have it's own challenges and obstacles, so building in sections breaks the job down into more easily manageable parts. Another advantage in building in sections is that you won't have to crawl through the fence as much during construction which can become very tiresome. You can simply walk around a shorter section of fence as necessary.

To keep the fence line as straight as possible, use string or twine to lay out your fence line on the ground before construction. Attach the string to a stake driven into the ground at one end of your fence line and then stretch it to the other end of the fence as tight as possible. This reveals the line that you will follow when marking your post locations on the ground.

---

**Handy Tip...**
**Polypropylene hay baling twine makes an excellent fence building twine for laying out long fence sections. It is cheap, strong, and comes in very long rolls. Always keep a spare roll or two on hand to use around your property as the need arises.**

---

If your property has dips and hills along the fence line, you will have to follow the natural lay of the property to some extent. Your fence can become unsightly if the rise and fall of top the fence line is too extreme in a short distance. If this is the case, it may be better to smooth out the rise and fall of the top of the fence line by adjusting the heights of your posts when installing them in the ground. One handy tip is to use string or twine attached to the tops of your posts to temporarily see what the completed fence will look like when finished and adjust your post heights up or down accordingly, till you get a smooth and graceful line along the top of the fence.

## *Barbed Wire Fences*

A simple barbed wire fence is probably the most successfully utilized fence in modern history. It's advantage is that it is relatively low cost to build using few materials, it is quick to build, and if properly constructed, will hold a wide variety of livestock. The biggest disadvantage of a barbed wire fence is that it will not contain or exclude smaller animals, varmints, dogs, wild hogs, etc. A barbed wire fence needs to be about 4 1/2 feet to 5 feet tall and contain at least 5 strands of wire. Because it relies on tension of the strands of wires to do it's job, heavy and strong corner posts are needed as anchor points. Gate posts, if needed, should be of the same strong construction also.

The interior posts can be simple metal t-posts, or wooden posts, or a combination of the two. Again, it is probably wise to measure the typical fence post spacing of other fences built in you local area, and use the same spacing for your posts.

While not absolutely necessary, twist on wire stays between each sets of posts will greatly help in keeping the barbed wire strands from sagging over time in the future. Heavy leather gloves and eye protection are imperative for protection from the razor sharp barbs on the wire. Also, it is necessary to use your fence stretcher discussed earlier to tighten each strand. This can be a dangerous job if the wire slips and whips out of position before you attach it to the posts.

---

**Handy Tip...**
**Using brightly colored spray paint, you can easily mark your fence post locations on the ground as you walk along and measure with your measuring tape.**

---

Once you have all of your post locations marked out, you now know the exact number of posts that you will need to build your fence. It's always prudent to purchase a few extra posts just in case of problems, as these posts can be stored away and used elsewhere on your property when needed.

The first steps in the construction of a barbed wire fence are the installation of the corner posts and/or end posts. If gates are going to be used at some place along the fence line, then the end posts on each side of the gate should be installed during this initial construction phase also. This gives you strong anchor points from which to stretch the barbed wire strands.

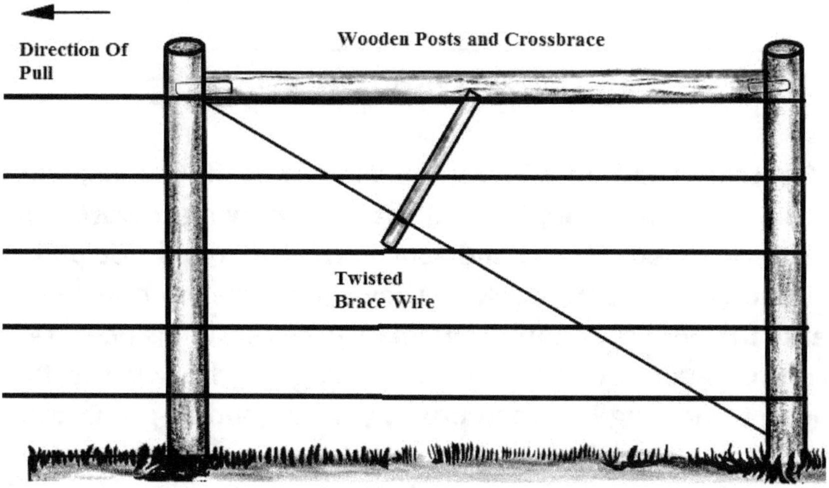


*Typical Fence End Brace*
*(Note the direction of pull to the twisted wire brace.)*

The next step is the installation of all of the interior posts along the fence line. Use your post driver to drive your metal t-posts into each spot that you marked earlier with spray paint. If you are using wooden posts, you will need to dig the post holes and set the posts in the ground.

Attach the first strand of barbed wire to one end corner post and then stretch the wire tightly at the other end. After stretching, nail or clip the barbed wire to the posts. It is always best to start with the lowest strand of wire first and work your way up to the final top strand. This is because you will be stepping from one side of the fence line to the other side many times while you are attaching the wire to the posts. This avoids having to stoop and crawl under the top wires if you had installed them first.

The final touch in construction of your new fence will be installing the the wire stays between each set of interior fence posts. These simply twist on in a screw-like fashion to help support and brace the barbed wire strands.

---

## How Tight Is Tight Enough?

**Stretching barbed wire can be dangerous. If it snaps, you will have a huge ball of tangled and sharp wire flying towards you at breakneck speed! Most hand fence stretchers will not pull wire with enough force to break it. They can easily slip however, and release the wire suddenly. How much wire tension is necessary? It mainly depends on it's length. As long as the wire is taught enough to not sag between posts, you're good to go. Eventually the wire will stretch even more on it's own after a few months anyway. There is really no such thing as a permanently tight barbed wire fence.**

---

## *Field Wire Fences*

A field wire fence is constructed very similarly to a barbed wire fence, but instead of using barbed wire, rolls of wire mesh are stretched between the corner posts and end posts.

The fence construction for the posts is virtually the same process and layout as a barbed wire fence. Rolls of field wire can be purchased at most home centers or farm supply stores and feed stores in your area.

There are many types of mesh designs to choose from and heights of the rolls will vary also. When choosing a mesh design, take into account what animals that you intend for the fence to contain or exclude. A standard all-purpose field wire will usually have mesh openings around 5 or 6 inches with smaller mesh opening near the bottom to prevent small animal entry. Roll heights of 49 inches are fairly standard. Since this height of fence is usually too short for most animal fences, you must add two or three strands of barbed wire above the top of the mesh wire to bring the total fence height up to around 5 feet. The strands of barbed wire will provide additional protection to deter cows, horses, and other large animals from trying to climb over the fence.

---

**Handy Tip...**

**If necessary, you can overlap two types of field wire. For example, you can run poultry mesh at the bottom of a field wire mesh fence to help contain chickens along with other larger animals.**

---

Field wire fences have many advantages over other fence styles. They will last a very long time if properly maintained. They do a great job of keeping destructive wild hogs, stray animals and livestock, and other harmful wildlife from entering your property.

A field wire fence also presents itself as a significant visual barrier for humans too, if constructed to a sufficient height and topped with several strands of barb wire.

Unfortunately, a field wire fence has several significant drawbacks that may deter you from choosing this design. The biggest drawback is cost. Field wire can be very expensive. A typical roll is around 330 feet long and will cost several hundred dollars per roll, depending on your local area.

Another drawback is that field wire makes a great trellis upon which vines, weeds, tree saplings love to attach themselves to, and they will quickly take over a field wire fence line. To keep a field wire fence clean of unwanted overgrowth takes a diligent commitment of regular spraying, trimming, and maintenance, when compared to a barbed wire fence design, for example. If you slack off with the upkeep, and vines and overgrowth do take over, it is virtually impossible to clear out the damage and try to salvage the wire mesh. In most cases the wire mesh must be completely removed, discarded, and replaced.

Layout and construction of a field wire fence is nearly the same as a barbed wire fence. The biggest difference is that you need a wire mesh type of stretcher to pull the length of mesh tight before attaching to the fence posts. This is usually constructed of a wooden beam with adjustable clamps attached to it. The design allows you to pull the wire mesh evenly without distorting the mesh out of shape.

Because a roll of wire mesh can be heavy and bulky to handle, it is usually necessary to have at least two people available to build a field wire fence. It is also advisable to purchase all of the rolls you will need for a fence project at once because they can often vary in appearance slightly from between production runs, or have availability delays, and it looks odd to mix different mesh styles in the same fence line.

Make sure your fence posts are all set close to the exact height required, as the mesh itself is a fixed height, and it is not adjustable. It is also advisable to have at least two strands of barbed wire on top of the mesh for fence protection and the barbed wire can be adjusted somewhat for slight fence post height variations if needed.

## Selecting The Appropriate Field Wire

### Field Wire Mesh

General purpose mesh for standard field fencing. Good for cattle, goats, hogs, etc. Must be topped with two or three strands of barbed wire to be effective and deter climbing.

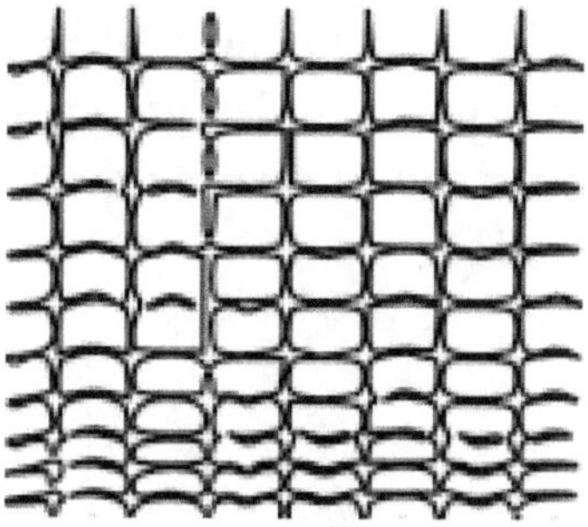

### V - Mesh

Useful for horse fencing. V-mesh deters horses from getting their hooves caught inside the mesh.

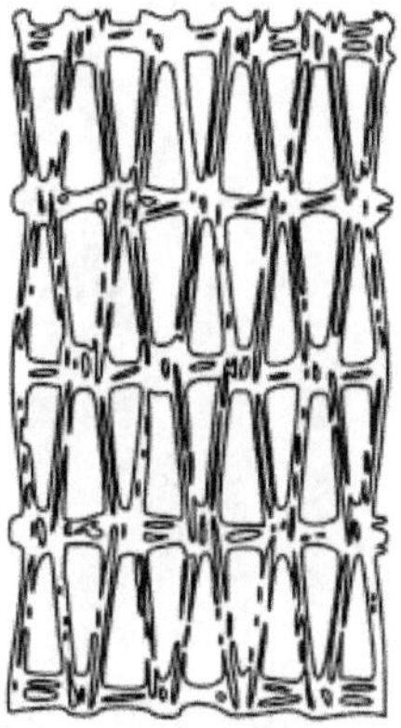

### Poultry Mesh

Generally used for fencing chickens or other birds. The mesh is small and constructed of light weight wire.

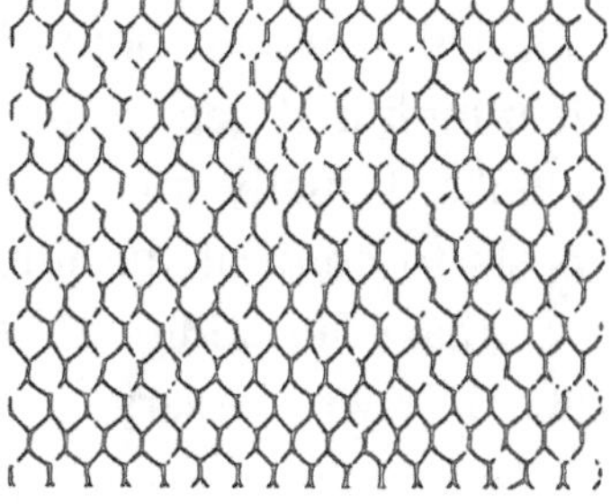

## *Board Fences*

A nicely built traditional white board fence stretching out along gently rolling terrain can look very pretty and traditional. The look is classic, and most often associated with horse farms and large rural estates. The design has been around for hundreds of years because it was the prevailing aesthetic back then, and the style has endured till today.

This style of fence is nearly always constructed completely of wood with wooden posts and cross boards. The wood must be pressure treated to prevent premature decay or some rot resistant species of wood should be used. Board fences are generally about 5 feet high and depending on use, will have four or five rows of cross planks. Usually a cover board is screwed over the front side of the posts to conceal the joints between the boards. Many board fences will have an additional flat horizontal top cap, although this is not absolutely necessary.

Board fences, like other fence styles, have advantages and disadvantages. Their biggest advantage is when they are well constructed, they can look beautiful. A board fence can frame a country estate and make a strong statement. The look is classic and if your property has a grand and classic look, a board fence would be appropriate. Even more so if you have an older classic style home in public view. Another advantage is that board fences are usually much gentler on livestock than barbed wire. If you are considering raising horses, this is especially important as they will not rip their skin and snag their long manes on a board fence when compared to a barbed wire fence.

Board fences unfortunately have many of the same disadvantages as a field wire fence. Costs can be enormous, and installation is very labor intensive. A board fence will also have the same overgrowth problems of a field wire fence and will require diligent maintenance. Board fences can quickly become coated in an unsightly green moss and mold when built under certain species of trees, such as Mulberry trees for example.

---

**Handy Tip...**

**A small gasoline powered chainsaw will be a time saver for cutting fence boards. Rough cuts caused by the chainsaw blade are acceptable. These joints will be hardly visible from a distance anyway.**

---

Board fence construction layout is the same as any other fence type. The spacing between the posts will be strictly dictated by the length of boards that you choose. It will be likely that each board may be an inch or two different in length and each will need to be trimmed during construction. Always use weather resistant screws instead of nails when possible. Nails tend to back out of their holes over time and the protruding nail heads can present a significant hazard to animals.

If you choose to paint your completed fence, use a small 6 inch paint roller for the broad areas of the fence and use a paintbrush to get paint into the various nooks and crevices that the roller will not reach. It is advisable to use a special purpose fence paint which is usually thicker and has special additives blended into the paint to help withstand mold and hold up to weather extremes better than normal house paint. This paint can be commonly found at farm supply stores.

---

**Lumber For Board Fencing**

**Use only pressure treated lumber or other rot-resistant species of wood. Typically board fences are constructed of rough-cut corral boards. Available at most rural lumber supply houses, these boards are pressure treated and sized to be a full 1 inch thick. They have a rough-sawn surface and can very slightly in their appearance and exact size. The differences in sizes and appearance from board to board is not usually visible from a distance. Available lengths can vary, so it is wise to check on availability and purchase your boards before setting the fence posts. This will ensure that the end joints on the boards fall at a fence post location.**

---

## *Garden Fencing*

Fences for gardens are usually fairly easy to construct. The main reason for a garden fence is to keep unwanted animals from eating your delicate garden plants. Rabbits, raccoons, and other varmints will help themselves, usually at night, and can cause significant damage to your garden. Deer can also be a problem, and if they are prevalent in your area, a much more robust fence will be required as a deer can jump over a 6 foot high fence with ease.

One thing to consider when planning and laying out a garden fence is ease of access for tractors, tillers, mowers and other power equipment that will be needed for garden maintenance. You do not want to build a fence too close to the perimeter of your garden keeping you from being able to maneuver equipment around inside your garden. Allow room for a full size garden tractor to turn around at the ends of the garden rows if you plan on using a tractor in your garden. Likewise, be sure to utilize a full size gate at an appropriate place in the fence line to allow for occasional vehicle entry such as a dump truck full of compost. If you just want to grow a small kitchen garden, then your fence design can be just a small temporary fence because you will probably move and expand your garden from time to time in another locations on your property. Electric fencing can also be utilized and will be discussed in detail in another section of this book.

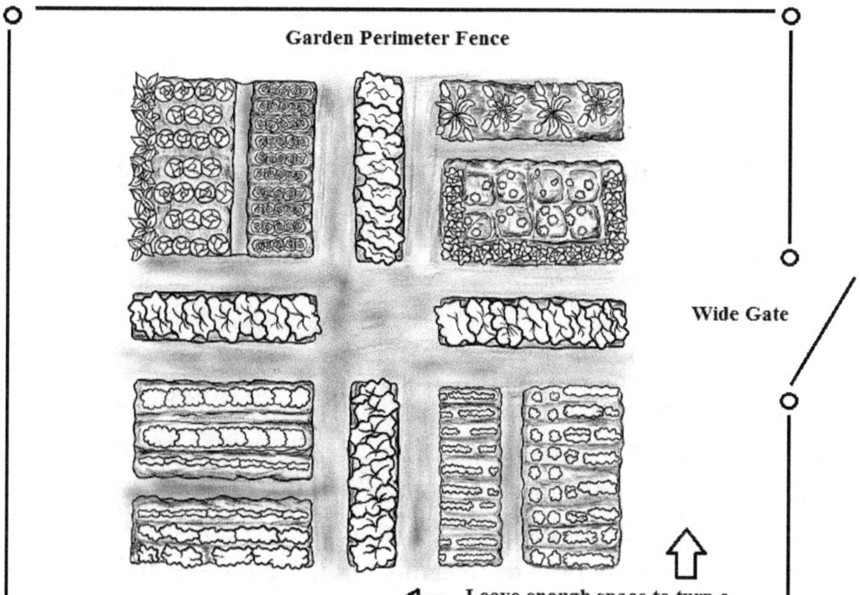


*Garden Fence Layout With Access Gate*

Posts for garden fences can generally be smaller and lighter than what is used in a typical property fence. Metal t-posts are an excellent choice for garden fences. The fence should be constructed with wire mesh. Use mesh wire that has a very small mesh size, as this can be usually successful in keeping larger snakes out of your garden.

If you are constructing a more permanent style of garden fencing to keep out deer, then you must plan on larger posts and possibly two rows of mesh wire stacked one on top of the other to bring the height up to approximately 8 feet.

Gates for deer resistant fencing must also be appropriately tall also. An electric wire, or two, strung around the outside of your garden fence can be a deterrent for many animals to keep them from digging under your fence or trying to climb over the top of the fence as raccoons often do.

---

**Handy Tip**

**If you are concerned about snakes in your garden, spreading sulfur powder around your rows and plants will help deter most snakes. After a rain, it will necessary to re-apply, as the sulfur is water soluble**

---

## *Animal Fencing*

Various breeds of farm animals may require special consideration when building animal pens, corrals, and holding areas. For example, goats and sheep will require a tight and tall fence to keep them from jumping over the top of the fence. Cattle can be especially powerful and destructive when upset or nervous and a heavy welded steel pipe fence would be the best choice for their corrals and working pens.

Horses tend to get their front hooves hung inside the mesh of a field wire fence. Various options of horse-safe fencing have been designed with a v-shaped mesh that helps prevent this problem.

Hogs are well known for digging and rooting under fences, so a strand or two of heavy barbed wire can be buried in the ground just below a mesh wire fence to deter them from digging there. When selecting a fence style for containing various animals, take into consideration the habits and temperament of the animal. The fence needs to be strong enough to contain the animals, and constructed in a manner that is safe for the animals to prevent their injury.

Small fenced areas commonly called "pens" need to be sized large enough so that the animals enclosed inside do not feel crowded or cramped due to the lack of interior space. This can lead to panicking and cause the animals to try to over-run or jump over the fence leading to escape or injury.

## *Electric Fencing*

Electric fences have become popular in recent years as they are affordable, easy and quick to construct, and to move as the need arises. Most often, these types fences will be temporary in nature, until a more permanent and suitable fence can be erected. Also, temporary electric fences can be a good choice if you intend to move animals to different areas for seasonal grazing for a few weeks or months at a time. The fence can easily be taken down and reassembled in a new location so that animals can be moved around your property.

Electric fences are more appropriately used as a temporary fencing solution due to their disadvantages. Their biggest disadvantage is that a typical electrical fence will do a poor job of containing or excluding all animals. Cows and horses may stay inside, but a wild hog will just ignore the shocks and walk through the fence. Varmints such as rabbits, raccoons, and other small animals will soon learn to jump through an electric fence without impunity. Another significant disadvantage with electric fences is the risk of starting a wildfire. During a drought, dry or brown grass that touches the wires can cause sparks and this can be extremely dangerous.

Finally, another significant hazard is the risk to humans. Touching an electric fence can be very painful and dangerous with the electric shock, especially if you have small or curious children around the fence.

Electric fences are designed to use an electric fence controller that supplies the electricity to the fence wires or mesh. These chargers should be designed to apply voltage in one second increments to allow for an animal or human who touches the fence to release and have time to escape to avoid a fatal electrocution. These controllers are commonly available in both standard 110 volt AC powered and solar-battery powered, which is useful in remote locations without electricity nearby. If your electric fence controller is solar powered, be sure to mount the solar panel unit in an area that receives maximum direct sunlight, facing a due south direction in order for the solar panel to capture as much sunlight as possible during the day.

At night, these units utilize an internal battery for power that is recharged during the day by the solar panel. Most modern fence controllers have sufficient power to operate a typical small to medium sized rural electric fence. Larger units are available, but they are costly and unnecessarily large for most rural homeowner situations.

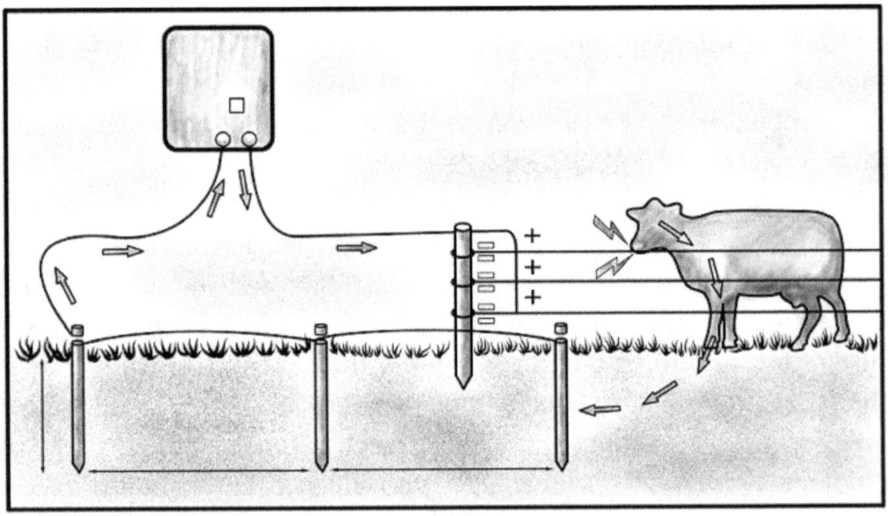


*Electric Fence Circuit*

Building an electric fence can be as simple as driving or pushing a few t-posts into the ground, attaching plastic insulators to the posts, and stringing up the light galvanized fence wire a few feet from the ground. Usually 3 strands will suffice with more or less depending on your particular situation. The fence controllers are usually weatherproof and easily mounted on a fence post nearby for easy connection to the fence wires. A ground rod must be placed near the controller to complete the electrical circuit. This rod can be driven into the ground like a t-post, or a hole dug and the rod placed inside the hole like a wooden post. Turn on the power to the controller and check your fence wires for electrical pulses with a special electric fence checker. Generally, these are a small handheld electrical device that touches the bare wire and flashes a small light bulb with each fence pulse. These devices are indispensable for diagnosing fence problems such as shorts, open circuits, or the strength of the pulses at long distances from the controller.

Electric fences work on a basic electrical circuit principal. This circuit delivers electrical energy to one or more fence wires. At the controller mounting location, a ground rod driven deep into the ground is the other side of the circuit. When an animal touches the fence wires, the circuit is completed to ground and they receive the shock pulses until they move away from the fence and the circuit is open again.

It is very important to keep a close watch on your animals when they encounter an electric fence for the first time. The shock will be quite alarming, so you will want to make sure that they don't get hung up in the fence trying to get away from it. After a few initial shocks, most animals quickly learn to avoid the fence altogether and rarely touch it again. Sometimes they will graze very close to the wire, but they instinctively know not to touch it once that they have been shocked.

Also, inspect the fence daily, if possible, for tall dry grass or limbs that have fallen from trees and are making shorted connections with the wires.

Of course, make sure to de-energize the fence anytime you are working near it, and don't forget to turn it back on when you are finished working or the fence will not work and be ineffective.

---

## Cattle Panels

Cattle panels are welded wire panels that are usually 16 ft long and 50 inches tall. These panels are stiff and will stand upright when needed. They typically come in several different mesh sizes and styles. There are many handy uses for cattle panels around any rural property. It is always a good idea to have several spare cattle panels available for use when necessary.

They are excellent for emergency fence repair. Simply place the panel up against the damaged section of fence and wire it into position to secure your fence. They can be later removed when you have the time to complete a more permanent fence repair.

They are also very handy for making a temporary fence around a kitchen garden, or even for making a trellis in the garden for climbing plants. Simply drive two t-posts into the ground and wire the panel upright between the posts. Another use for cattle panels is blocking access to barns and sheds to keep unwanted animals out or in as the case requires.

Cattle panels are readily available from farm supply stores or feed stores and building supply houses. One thing to keep in mind, is that you will either need to have the panels delivered from the store, or transport them yourself using a suitable trailer because they are stiff in shape and cannot be rolled up. They are typically too large to fit in the bed of most standard trucks.

---

Building fences around your land is one of the most important tasks you will do as a rural landowner. Whether you just own a few acres in a rural subdivision, or if you have many acres in a remote location, fences will be necessary for your privacy, security, and the safety and containment of your animals. Fences can be very important also for the exclusion of wild animals and stray livestock that could cause significant damage to your property. Choosing an appropriate fence style and learning to build a strong and straight fence is a task that must be considered carefully.

# Key Points..

Purchase basic fence building tools.
Consider buying or renting a motor style auger.
If building a field wire fence, select the appropriate field wire for the specific need.
Always use pressure treated lumber for board fencing.
Select the appropriate style of fencing for various animals.
Electric fencing should be considered temporary fencing and checked and maintained carefully.

# Chapter 2
# Gates

Gates are an integral part of any fence. On a typical rural property there will be a main entrance gate at the beginning of your driveway or access road, as well as vehicle gates for the various cross fences, and pasture areas. You will probably have small walk-through gates in fenced areas that receive a lot of foot traffic such as next to a barn or building. Gates have much in common with the fences that they are attached to. For example, a gate on a field wire fence must also have mesh wire incorporated into the gate design itself. Otherwise, savvy animals will just step through the open gate rails and pass through the fence line with ease. Tall fences, or high game fences, will also need an appropriately tall gate for the same reasons. Entrance gates will need to be secure to prevent unwanted entry, but they will also need to be opened easily for frequent use. The biggest problems associated with most gate installations are the physical weight of the gate that causes sagging, or the width of the gate is insufficient to allow for passage of larger equipment, therefore causing damage both to the gate and the equipment trying to pass through. A good gate installation takes planning and the extra effort that is sometimes required to make the gate sufficiently strong and durable.

## *Property Entrance Gates*

These types of gates are usually installed at the beginning of your driveway or property entrance road and they will typically serve multiple purposes. They must exclude unwanted foot or vehicle traffic onto your property. Sometimes they must keep unwanted stray animals out, while simultaneously keeping your animals contained inside your property. Often, they can are decorative in their design and construction and provide a nice visual entrance to your home and property. A entrance gate is also likely to be the most used gate on your property, so it should be very durable and easy to open, close, and keep secured.

An often overlooked aspect of entrance gate design is the size or width required. If this is the only outside gate on your property, then everything must pass through that gate. Larger service vehicles, the occasional delivery vehicle, tractors and equipment, etc. must all pass through that entrance gate. It has to be a sufficient width to let them through. (An alternate solution to this problem could be an additional double gate somewhere along the property to use for the occasional over-sized vehicle to pass through to avoid any risk of damage to the main gate.)

The minimum opening width of an entrance gate on a rural property should be at least 16 feet. You can use a single 16 foot gate, or two 8 foot gates in a double opening gate arrangement. One thing to consider is a bit of the total width is lost because of the installation of the hinge posts for the gate(s).

# *Standard Steel Tube Entrance Gates*

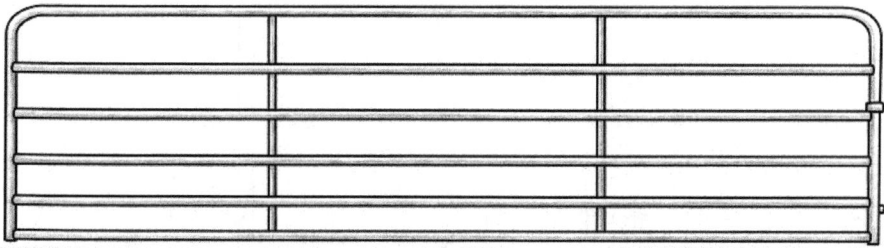

An entrance gate can be easily installed by any homeowner if using a typical steel tube gate commonly offered at home centers or farm supply stores. The advantages of these types of gates are their low cost, relatively easy and quick availability, and their light weight. These gates are constructed of thin wall steel tubing and are surprisingly light in weight. One person can usually handle the gate installation without much effort. Their disadvantages are that they tend to rust easily and strong animals such as cattle can push against them and bend them out of shape. The most basic installation would be a single gate hung between two gate posts on hinge pins and secured with a short section of chain.

As long as the gate is secure enough to keep animals from passing through the bars, then your job is complete. If needed, a small section of left-over field wire mesh can be attached to the gate to keep smaller animals from passing through the gate rails. Better yet, many tube gates are available with a steel mesh already welded into the gate structure and these would be an excellent choice to compliment a field wire fence.

## *Welded Steel Entrance Gates*

A welded gate can usually be purchased from a local welding shop ready-made or they can be custom fabricated to your specifications. The advantages of welded gates are their strength, appearance, and they are very durable and can last for many years. Styles can range from quite elaborate designs, to as simple as you prefer. Often a gate will have what is known as a "ranch style entrance," that incorporates tall gateposts on each side of the gate with a center beam overhead connecting these posts. This design was initially created to help brace the end posts and prevent heavy wooden gates from sagging from their weight. Nowadays most ranch style entrances are made of welded pipe for strength and are mostly decorative in design.

---

**Handy Tip...**

**If you build a ranch style gate entrance with a center beam, make sure that it is high enough so that tall vehicles such as RV's or 18-wheelers or firetrucks can safely pass underneath.**

---

Their disadvantages are their cost and their weight. A custom welded gate can easily cost several thousand dollars, depending on it's design complexity. These gates can also weigh several hundred pounds when completed. Installation will most often require onsite welding and cutting and the heavy steel gateposts will need to be cemented into the ground to handle their extra weight.

## *Wooden Entrance Gates*

A wooden entrance gate can be constructed to look very attractive and unique. These gates are usually built as a double-opening gate style as the wood tends to be heavy and prone to sagging over time. Sagging can be alleviated somewhat by using two smaller center opening gates instead of one very long single gate.

Wooden gates are usually not available commercially anymore, and therefore must be constructed or contracted by the homeowner. The advantages are that wooden gates can be styled exactly to your own tastes and they can look very traditional and attractive, especially if you are using a traditional wooden fence next to the gate.

They are typically cheap and easy to build, using basic carpenter skills and tools.

A wooden gate's disadvantage is it's weight. Wood is heavy, and unless they are constructed in a robust manner, they will easily sag under their own weight over time. They also must be painted and maintained regularly, just the same as a wooden fence.

## *Gaps*

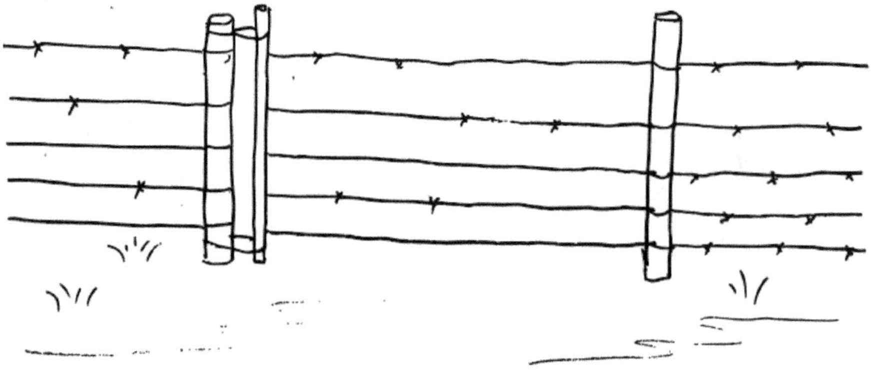

The lowly gap is a poor substitute for a proper gate, but it is still widely used as a temporary gate because it is very easy, quick, and cheap to set up. A gap is a gate that is constructed of strands of wire attached to the corner post of a fence on one side, and the other end is connected to a free-floating post or stick. To use a gap you pick up the stick that is free floating and walk it over to the other adjacent corner post. And by using a short piece of wire, you tie it to that corner post in an upright position. This effectively creates a small section of fence between the two corner posts. The wire strands will be somewhat loose and saggy and a twist-on wire stay or two will help keep them evenly spaced. The gap is surprisingly effective against cattle and horses when constructed of barbed wire.

## *Manual Entrance Gate Mechanicals*

The simplest gate latch design is a short section of chain wrapped around the gate and a gatepost and further secured by a padlock. This may be sufficient for a quick short-term solution, but you will soon get tired of having to physically get out of your vehicle to unlock and open, drive through and then close and lock the gate. This will be especially so in rainy or snowy weather. Nevertheless, this simple chain and lock arrangement is easy, and foolproof and secure. If preferred, mechanical gate locking mechanisms can be purchased to avoid having to use a chain. Keep in mind that these mechanical locks still require you to exit your vehicle to operate them manually.

If you have built a wooden gate, these types of gates are usually secured by a sliding wooden board incorporated into the gate design very similar to the old style barn door latches. The gates will still need a way to lock and secure them from being opened.

---

### Entrance Gate Operation

**An entrance gate is the most used gate on your property, so it is wise to consider ease of operation and convenience for use in every kind of weather. It should be secure for safety and it should be durable in it's mechanical design. While seemingly simple, these can be some tall requirements that need be considered carefully to avoid problems.**

---

A few words about padlocks for entrance gates; If you have multiple family members, they will probably each want their own key, so be sure to have additional keys made when you purchase the padlock. Combination locks tend to freeze up in cold weather and are not as durable as key style padlocks. Also combination locks have a tendency to allow rainwater to seep inside the lock body causing internal corrosion of the lock itself that will cause premature failure.

If you need to have your property accessible to workers, service people, outsiders etc., they may require their own separate lock and key. Most commercial welding shops know how to construct an "oilfield gate latch," whereas the design will allow attachment of multiple padlocks so each entity can come and go with their own specific padlock and key as required, without disrupting the other padlocks.

## *Electric Gate Mechanicals*

Electrically operated gate mechanisms have become ubiquitous to rural properties in recent years because of their convenience. Many companies now market electric gate opener kits that the average homeowner can easily self-install. These kits are usually adaptable to a wide variety of gate styles and sizes. For double opening gate arrangements, they also offer kits that will employ two gate actuator arms, one for each gate, that are simultaneously operated by a single gate controller.

Regardless of the style of opener that you choose, electric gate openers have some advantages and disadvantages. Their biggest advantage, by far, is convenience. Most electric gates have remote control buttons similar to a garage door opener. Many newer automobiles also have the remote controls already built into the vehicle's electronics package. You simply drive up to the gate and click the button and the gate opens automatically while you remain in your vehicle, out of the weather. Once you drive through the open gate, you can close it yourself with another button click, or most models of gate openers will have a self closing timer feature. You can also purchase an accessory electronic locking mechanism that will secure your gate from unauthorized entry.

The biggest disadvantage of electric gate openers is that they tend to have many mechanical moving parts that require frequent maintenance.

They also have electronic control boxes which contain delicate circuit boards that can easily be damaged from intruding insects or lightning strikes nearby. If you have a large and heavy welded steel gate, or a custom gate design, then you would be better off to have a professional install a commercial style of electric gate opener to reliably handle the extra weight.

These styles can also sometimes accommodate a large sliding gate. This style of gate slides off to one side of the fence on a chain-and-roller arrangement, and their advantage is that they can operate very large and heavy gates with ease, versus trying to swing open a heavy gate on hinges, which can be problematic. In these specialized cases, a professional install would be a better choice because on-site welding and cement work will be involved.

For a typical rural swing gate, an electric gate opener operates with two main components; the gate actuator arm that moves the gate itself, and an electronic controller that contains the electrical circuit components. Before you purchase a homeowner installed gate opener kit, you should take into consideration the style, physical length, and weight of your gate. With this information in hand, you can then purchase an electric opener kit that will properly sized to meet your needs. When selecting a particular kit, the manufacturer's specifications will contain the maximum weight and length that the gate actuator motor can safely and reliably operate.

---

**Handy Tip...**

**If you purchase several electric gate openers for various gates over a period of time, try to stick with the same brand if possible. This will allow you to swap parts between openers as necessary, for temporary repairs. Most gate parts are usually interchangeable and it's convenient to build up a set of spare parts that can be used on any of your electric gates as needed.**

---

One specification to consider is how to supply electric power to the gate opener mechanism. Electric gate openers generally get their power from either standard 110V AC power that you must supply to the gate, or they can be solar powered via a solar panel and battery arrangement. In a worst case scenario, they can also operate from a simple 12V DC battery that you must periodically re-charge yourself as necessary.

The advantage of using 110V AC power is reliability. The gate opener has to have a good strong source of electrical power in order to operate reliably, and supplying 110V AC power assures that. The disadvantage of using this choice is that it can be expensive to bury an electrical cable all the way from the nearest power source to the gate itself. In some cases, it may be impossible because of the distances involved.

If this is your situation, you want to choose to use a gate opener that can operate on a 12V DC battery. This allows for you to use a solar panel to charge the battery or just remove the battery and charge it yourself when necessary. The advantages with this method are ease of installation and cheaper costs when compared to burying an electrical cable from a distant power source. The disadvantage of using solar/battery power is that the solar panel must be sized large enough to adequately charge the battery reliably and it is imperative that the solar panel is mounted in an area of maximum direct sunlight. If your gate is in a shady area with many trees, this can be a problem.

Regardless of what power supply method you ultimately choose, the reliability of an electric gate opener is wholly dependent on having an adequate supply of electrical power every day, year after year. For example, if your gate is solar/battery powered, the sun may not shine adequately during the snowy winter months and the battery will eventually become discharged and the electric opener will cease working. Or another example, if your opener runs on 110V AC power and you live in an area that experiences frequent power outages, the gate will not open if the main electrical power to your property is out.

Overall, in spite of the technical challenges that can sometimes happen, an electric gate opener is a wonderful convenience and is useful addition to your property.

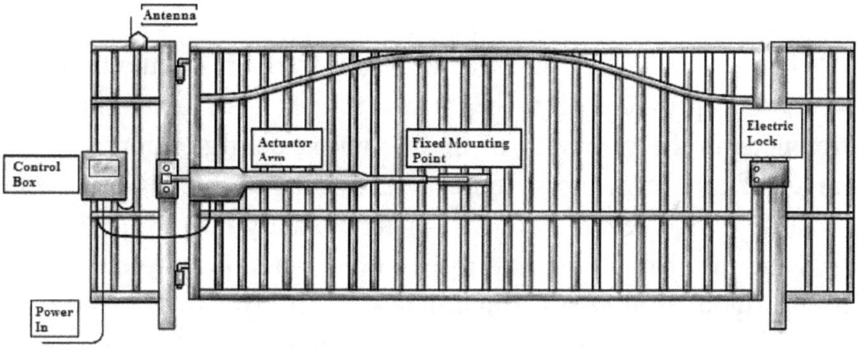


*Typical Electric Gate Layout*

## *Electric Gate Opener Installation*

After purchasing your new electric gate opener kit, read the instructions thoroughly and familiarize yourself with the overall design and installation as presented in the instructions. Usually gate opener companies will provide additional online instructional videos which can be most helpful if you run into a problem during installation. While the various brands differ somewhat, they all have adopted the same basic principles in design. A small electric motor drives a screw actuator arm attached to both the fixed gatepost and the gate itself. When this arm contracts or expands in length, the gate opens or closes. The electronic controls may be enclosed in a separate box or sometimes they are enclosed in the actuator arm as a sealed unit. A space for a small 12V DC auxiliary battery is usually provided for power.

If your unit is solar powered, then you will have a separate small solar panel to mount facing due south if possible in an area of the most direct sunlight.

Often, you will have to mount this solar panel some distance away from the gate controller itself, especially if there are large trees obstructing the view of the sun. If this is your case, you will need to provide a small extra length of 2-conductor stranded wire in order to attach the solar panel to the controller.

When installing the gate actuator arm, pay close attention to the instructions provided by the manufacturer. For example: small differences in the geometry of the mounting configuration will make a large difference in the speed at which the gate moves. The details and particulars of every gate will dictate exactly how you will install your actuator arm, so be sure to pay close attention to your actuator arm’s design and follow the instructions carefully.

If your gate is a center opening double gate style, then you will need to mount an actuator arm on each separate gate and also bury a small electric line under the road surface to connect the two actuator arms to the control box.

If you opted to purchase opener accessories such as a guest entry keypad, these will need to be mounted in a visible location that is preferably easily accessible from a car window for use.

Many folks choose a deluxe entry setup that includes multiple remote controls for the property owner, a gate code keypad for guests, and a magnetic vehicle detector to automatically open the gate when a guest approaches the inside of the gate when exiting the property. These accessories are wired into the proper terminals on the control board and are easy to add at a later date if needed. After your controller and any extra accessories are installed, and the actuator arm is mounted, power on the unit and prepare to adjust the actuator arm.

## Electric Gate Installation Checklist

☑ Make sure that your gate sits level between the gateposts when closed and also while fully open. By having a level gate, the actuator arm can do it's job of opening and closing smoothly without having to strain under the weight of an out-of-level gate. This is especially important if you have a heavy gate.

☑ When mounting the gate to the gateposts, make sure there are about 3 or 4 inches of clearance under the gate at all points, both when open and closed. If your gate rubs or drags the ground at any point, the opener will not work properly. The gate must be completely free swinging with no obstructions in it's path or binding in the hinges. If, for whatever reason, the gate cannot be raised for the proper clearance, then the soil will need to be scraped away under the gate.

☑ Mount your control box out of access from chewing animals. The same can be said for the electrical wires between the various gate opener components. Horses, cows, and goats, are curious by nature, and love to chew on wires etc.

☑ Theft of your gate opener should be considered. Electric openers are expensive and easy targets for thieves if they are mounted in secluded rural areas. Use a stout padlock to attach the actuator arm to it's mounting brackets on the gate instead of just bolts or pins. Next, use Torx head screws to mount the control box so that the average thief will not have the correct tool necessary to unscrew the control box from it's mounting. Try to mount your solar panel up as high as possible in an unobtrusive location. Having a very visible security camera at your entry gate is a strong deterrent to thieves and will be discussed in another section of this book.

Follow the manufacturer's instructions for exact adjustment details of the gate opener. The basic premise of most electric gates is to open the gate fully to allow wider vehicles to pass through. After a predetermined set time, the gate will automatically close. When the gate closes and approaches the end of it's swing to the gatepost, it will stop at a predetermined point, small enough that livestock will not pass through, yet avoiding physically slamming the gate into the gatepost and eventually damaging the actuator arm. Usually this stopping point is adjusted via a button on the circuit board and several attempts will likely be needed to get it adjusted just right. Take your time making the various adjustments and to get everything operating smoothly and reliably.

Electric gate openers can also be very convenient and helpful for your interior gates as well. For example; if you drive through several cross fenced pastures daily to feed your livestock, then having electric gates is a great work saver, especially in bad weather. Most often the installation is simplified somewhat, as guest access and security measures are not as important for interior gates that are intended for private use.

# Key Points...

A fence gate can be a useful and beautiful addition to any section of fence.

Gates can the ensure security of your property and the security of your animals. By following a few basic guidelines, your gate installation will be strong and long lasting.

Keeping gates maintained properly should a seasonal task and will prevent future problems.

Gate styles for a rural property can usually be classified into 4 different types, with each style having specific advantages and disadvantages.

Always keep in mind the maximum open width and the overhead height of an entrance gate, to allow entry for larger vehicles and equipment.

A typical electric gate can easily be installed by the average rural property owner. Having a clean and constant source of power to the electric gate controls is key to consistent operation all year long in any weather.

Be sure to follow the manufacturer's installation instructions. This will assure the proper mounting geometry and operation.

# Chapter 3

# Roads and Driveways

Building suitable roads and/or driveways around your property is a necessary step to gain access to the various places around your property. If you are purchasing raw land and nothing currently exists on your land at purchase, then you will likely just create paths naturally as you work around your property. Eventually this will cause damage and ruts to these areas and the subject of road building will become important. Entrance roads or driveways within your property will need special care as they will be used daily, while roads and paths to other areas can be built in the future, when the need arises. In this chapter, we will discuss building and maintaining a serviceable property entrance road and then these same concepts can be applied to other roads on your land, as needed.

Dirt or gravel roads are probably the simplest and cheapest roads to build and maintain on a rural property. Cement or asphalt is usually reserved for shorter driveways because of their higher costs and the benefits of appearance. Cement and asphalt work takes specialized knowledge and equipment, and therefore should be left to professionals to design and build. Gravel and dirt roads can easily be built by the average homeowner, as long as you understand the basic concepts of layout, compaction, drainage, and slope of your property. These four items will need to be addressed before you can build a suitable road on your land that will last for years with minimal maintenance and upkeep.

## *Layout and Clearing Pathways*

The first step in building an entrance road on your property is to consider the layout of your land and how you wish to drive into your property. Everybody's property is unique and different, but some key considerations are navigating your road around creeks or ditches, steep hillsides, and other natural obstacles. Often overlooked is deciding where to enter your property from the public road. You should consider things like finding a safe place on the public road to turn into your property. For example, if your entrance is in the middle a blind curve on the public road, you will always risk a higher danger of an accident each time you drive in and out of your property. If possible, take the time to observe the local traffic on the public road and plan your entrance location accordingly.

The interior of your property may present several obstacles as previously mentioned and therefore your road should be designed curve safely around these obstacles. When laying out curves in your proposed road path, keep in mind that at some point, you will be driving large equipment or pulling long trailers and these vehicles will need a wide path and gentle curves to safely navigate the road. A small and steeply winding road, while sometimes charming to look at, is rarely practical for everyday use.

If you need to navigate a steep hill, use switchbacks up the hill as you layout the road to avoid having long and steep paths that will invite erosion on steep hillsides during rainstorms.

Finally, try to keep your road layout in harmony with your natural property layout as much as possible. For example, if you have a rectangular or square property with no major obstacles, then a long perfectly straight road might be more attractive and practical than a curvy road for no apparent reason. Roads through woods or valleys and hillsides will require a curvy road that follows the easiest and most logical path to your home.

If necessary, trees will need to be cut and moved out of the way, and the left-over stumps removed completely out of the ground. Stump grinding is a process of using a grinder machine to pulverize the leftover tree stump into small wood chips. These machines can be rented or hired out at a reasonable cost. One thing to consider is that at some point a large depression will eventually form in the ground where each stump was located. This is due to rotting of the left-over wood chips over time, and a void forms where there was previously no soil. There really is no good solution for this except to try and remove as much of the wood chips as possible initially, then keep filling the depressions in the ground with firm soil till a flat surface eventually remains. Lastly, keep in mind that tree limbs overhanging the road may be a problem for taller vehicles, so these will need to be pruned and trimmed accordingly also.

## *Compaction*

In it's simplest terms, compaction is the result of driving heavy vehicles across your property till you reach a point that you start pushing the soil into ruts and creating a firm and hard surface. In road building, this is important because initially your soil may be loose and soft or perhaps rocky and rough, depending on your soil type. If you properly compact your road from the outset, then ruts will be minimized and the road surface will have a firm foundation and stay in place without eroding and sinking unevenly, creating potholes. By compacting your natural road surface before covering it with your final road material of choice, you will greatly reduce these problems. Compaction nearly always involves using equipment such as tractors and rollers. Without these tools, your job of compaction is more difficult, but suitable results can still be achieved by simply driving back and forth over the entire width and length of the road with your personal vehicle till the soil is tight and compacted.

## *Drainage*

Drainage of rainwater is probably the number one problem in the maintenance of a dirt road. Rainstorms and floods will happen eventually and all of that water needs to go somewhere - downhill. Even the flattest properties still need to carefully consider water drainage. The easiest solution is to employ ditches along each side of the road to handle excess water runoff. Ditches can be problematic if they are poorly designed. Ditches that are too deep are unsightly and can be difficult to mow and keep weed free. Ditches that are too wide and shallow will not move excess water very well and waste precious land area. Effective ditches are always a compromise between necessity and practicality. The best advice is to mentally visualize water runoff in a heavy rainstorm and where the water will be flowing when it encounters your road. Next, plan and cut ditches along each side of your road as necessary to move this excess water along the side or away from the roadbed until it eventually exits your property naturally. If your ditch is located on a steep hillside, you can slow down the water runoff by lining the ditch with heavy rocks which will aid in preventing erosion of the soil underneath. Again, effective ditches are a balance between what's the best design to move rainwater and what's best design for the easiest cleaning and maintenance of the ditch. Planning ahead will alleviate many future headaches.

## *Slope*

Slope is the overall drainage direction of your entire land from it's highest point till water exits your property. Even the flattest properties will have some minor slope. Knowing this overall direction is necessary in order to build a road that will accommodate the movement of water across your property. Water always flows downhill, of course. Roads can effectively create a dam if they are built up high enough to prevent this natural movement of water. This can become a problem and create wet and marshy areas that were once previously well drained. By using roadside ditches and routing your road properly to move water around the road to a naturally lower area on your property, you can avoid this problem.

## *Roadbase Materials*

There are many roadbase materials to choose from. The main deciding factors to consider are cost, availability, and what is the most appropriate for your property. There is no reason to re-invent the wheel, so take a drive around your local area and see what other folks are successfully using on their roads. If crushed limestone seems to be the material of choice in your area, then there is probably a good reason for that. If iron ore gravel seems to be prevalent, then it's probably easily available nearby.

Unfortunately, roadbase material can be very costly and can present itself as a major obstacle in your planning and selection. In many cases, your natural soil type on your property can be graded and used as a temporary substitute till you can afford a more suitable roadbed material. Sandy soil can easily be graded and shaped into a usable road. It's chief drawback is that it erodes very easily and thus requires constant grading to keep it in place. Natural clay can be used also. Compacting the clay as tight as possible when it is slightly moist will greatly help it shed rainwater and prevent creating a sticky mud bog. Rocky soil is the best natural roadbase material as the loose rocks in the soil naturally help prevent erosion of the roadbed. Again, compaction greatly helps to keep everything in place.

Regardless of what roadbase you are currently working with, the basic principles of shaping a road bed are the same. Most important is creating a crown in the center of the road. This means shaping and grading the road so that the center of the road bed is slightly higher than the sides. This makes rainwater drain completely off the roadbed and into the ditches alongside the road.

Keeping the roadbed as dry as possible and avoiding standing water on the roadbed itself, is key factor in preventing soft spots and potholes. A crown height of about 6 inches on a road that is about 10 feet wide is usually sufficient. If you make the crown too high and steep, you risk scraping the bottom of low clearance vehicles and making the road uncomfortable to navigate as your vehicle will have a tendency to roll off the edge of the road and into the ditch.

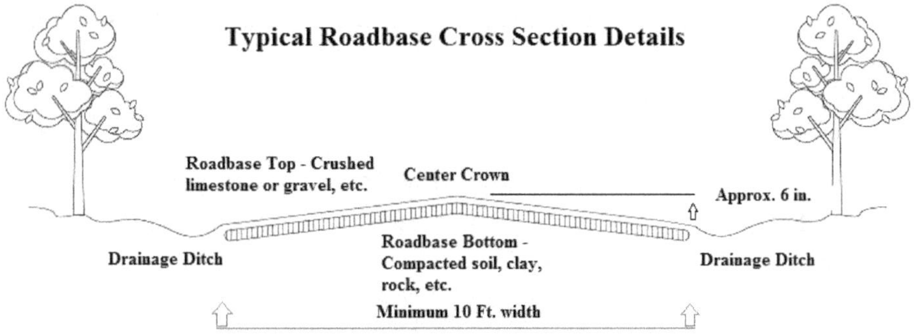


## *Grading a Dirt Road*

The best way to maintain a dirt or gravel road is to regularly grade or scrape it. Grading smooths the road surface and naturally fills in shallow dips and potholes. Gravel and rocks tend to eventually move to the edges of the road as you use it. Vehicle tires will push the rocks and soil away from the center and off to the sides, especially in curves. Periodic grading will move this material back into it's proper position on the surface of the roadbed and help keep the surface of the roadbed firm. Grading has to be done by machine on a long entrance road. If you have just a short driveway, then you can easily use a garden rake and keep your road in shape. Anything longer than a short driveway will require a tractor of some sort and a grader blade attachment or a box blade.

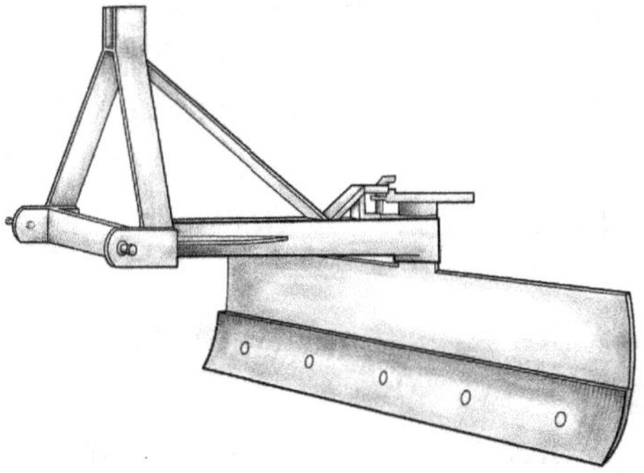

*Tractor Grader Blade*

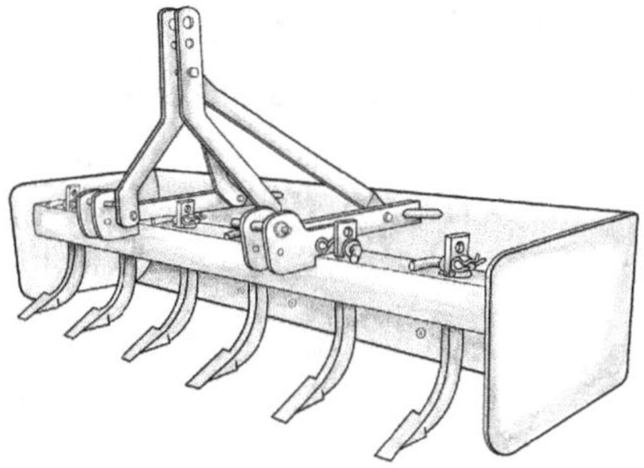

*Tractor Box Blade*

Both attachments do a similar job, but the grader blade is better for moving material that has washed away from the roadbed back into it's proper place. A grader blade attachment can usually be turned at an angle by it's design and this helps slide the roadbase material to the center of the roadbed as you drive along grading the road with your tractor.

A box blade usually stays square to the tractor and due to it's weight and enclosed sides, smoothes the road surface better than a grader blade. With a bit of practice, you will learn how to keep your dirt road smooth and crowned properly by grading on a regular schedule.

# Key Points...

Building and maintaining roads and driveways on your property is an important part of owning a rural property. Whether your entrance road is one mile long or just a short gravel driveway to your home, careful pre-planning and construction is paramount. Take into consideration important features such as layout, roadbase materials, drainage, and future maintenance.

Ditches should be a compromise between efficient water drainage and ease of mowing and maintenance.

Try to avoid creating a dam with a built-up roadbed that interferes with the overall slope and drainage of your property

Always grade a slight crown in the center of the roadbed to drain away standing water off of the road surface.

Road maintenance is necessary to keep potholes filled and to reshape the center crown for good water drainage off of the roadbase.

# Chapter 4
# Utilities and Easements

Basic utilities such as electricity, water, and sewer will be needed on your property. If you are planning to live "off-grid" you will still need these utilities for modern conveniences, but you will be installing and maintaining them yourself. Regardless, planning ahead will assure that any utilities and their associated easements on your property will not become cumbersome.

Additional utilities such as standby generators, solar power systems, and propane tanks will need to be considered also. Understanding how these utilities work and safely using them is an important part of rural living.

# Electricity

Electricity providers will supply power to your property via overhead power lines, or perhaps underground cables, to your chosen site on your property. Usually after you have obtained the proper civil permits, the electric company will send an engineer out to physically inspect your property. If possible, it is advisable to be present when they look at your property so that you can each discuss any particular property issues. After finding the best route into your property, the utility engineer will usually have paperwork ready for your signature, that describes an explicit "easement" on your property. While terms and conditions of easements can vary widely, an easement is basically a pathway on your land that the utility company can use for access for the installation and future maintenance of their infrastructure. If your property is secured with fences and gates, they will often times need an additional gate on the easement so that they can access for utility trucks and other maintenance equipment. Underground utilities will still need a designated easement over the underground cable also for the same reasons.

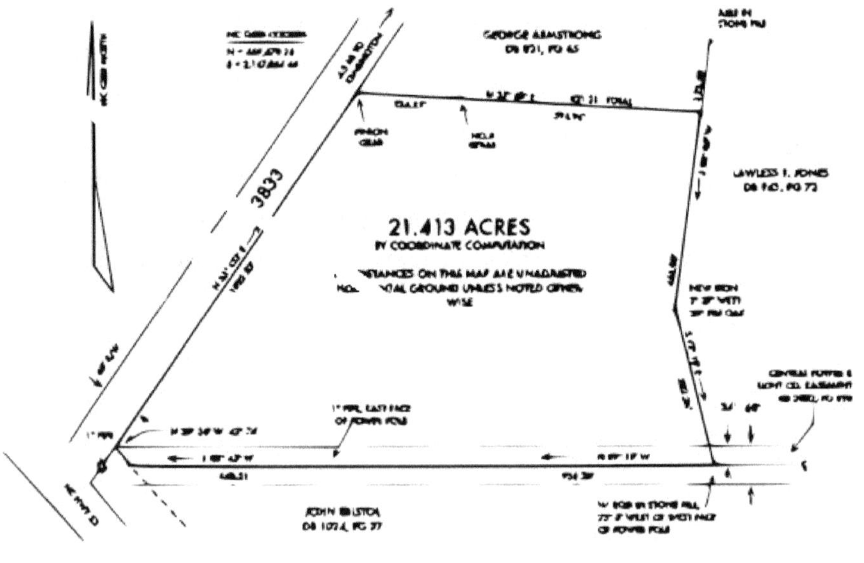

## Standby Generators

While discussing grid electrical services, the topic of standby generators should be included. These days, the reliability of the electrical grid is becoming increasingly unstable. For those living in a rural area, grid reliability seems to fail rather frequently during storm events. The use of electric generators for home emergency standby use has become an increasingly common practice.

Generators for home use can usually be classified into two main categories. One type is the permanently mounted whole-house type of generator. The other is a portable type of generator that is intended for a specific single use as compared to powering an entire house.

## Whole House Standby Generators

Whole house generators usually run on propane or natural gas for fuel. They have an automatic transfer switch. What this means is that they will automatically sense a power outage and start the generator motor. Next, they disconnect the house electrical circuits from the utility grid and transfer the electrical power from the generator to the house and you then have electrical power inside your house as usual. After the grid electrical power is restored, the generator transfers the house electrical circuits back to the grid power and then shuts down the generator motor. This whole process just takes a few seconds from sensing the initial power outage to getting power back through the generator.

Whole house generators have several benefits. As discussed, they start automatically with no fumbling in the dark looking for flashlights and trying to manually start a portable generator. You have a choice of natural gas or propane for fuel and there is no need to store cans of gasoline. Most rural property owners will choose to use propane. Finally, because they must be professionally installed, they tend to be safer than a portable generator.

Their disadvantages are the high initial purchase cost and further ongoing costs related to preventive maintenance which generally must be performed by a professional and not the homeowner themselves.

## *Portable Generators*

These smaller generators can be easily purchased through home centers and online in various sizes and styles. They will usually have a small gasoline engine attached to a generator which is bolted to an external frame assembly. Sometimes handles and wheels are attached to make moving the generator easy and safer for a single person. These generators will also have various styles of electrical receptacles. Some models will provide standard 110V power along with 220V also. Portable generators can easily be stored away out of the weather when not in use. Since they have no permanent connection to the house electrical circuits, a means must be provided to supply power to your house when needed. This can be very problematic and also very dangerous if done incorrectly.

It is highly recommended to have a professional licensed electrical contractor help you determine the size and type of portable generator that you will need. The largest issue is the size or wattage needed out of the generator itself. Rarely can a small portable generator produce enough power to run an entire house as normal. You must prioritize what items are crucial such as freezers, window AC units, etc., and which items can be eliminated during a prolonged power outage. A professional can look at your electrical breaker panel and determine which electrical circuits are vital. Then they can easily determine the proper size or wattage needed in a portable generator to provide power to these circuits only.

Another issue is the transfer switch. When a power outage occurs and a generator of any type is used, the power from the generator can back-feed into the electrical grid and electrocute the linemen working on the grid.

To avoid this dangerous situation, the house must first be completely disconnected from the power grid. Only then can auxiliary power from the generator be applied and used inside the house. This is normally done via a transfer switch, either manual or automatic. Portable generators generally use a manual transfer switch since they must be manually started by the homeowner.

A benefit of using a portable generator is the very low cost when compared to whole house standby generators. Another benefit is that the homeowner can perform their own maintenance such as oil changes etc. One benefit often not considered is that a portable generator is also handy for using in various remote places on your property when needed. For example, if you are building a fence on your property and you need electric power for your saws and other tools, a portable generator can be used on site.

The disadvantages are many, however. The main disadvantage is that during a typical power outage, you must first disconnect the transfer switch and then hook up the portable generator. Then you must manually start the generator and carefully apply the electrical power to only those vital circuits in your home while disconnecting any other circuits.

All of this must be done carefully and with some knowledge of how the electrical circuits in your home operate. Lastly, all of this is usually done in the dark during stormy weather. One additional note is that you must store cans of gasoline to resupply the generator as needed. During prolonged power outages, you will need a means to purchase additional gasoline which can be sometimes hard to find after major storm events.

Generators of either type are nearly a necessity these days on a rural property. They become even more important if you have elderly or sick people living with you who need access to electrical power for their medical equipment. Finally, aside from electrical grid issues, a portable generator can be very useful for general use around your property whenever needed. Take the time to determine your overall needs before choosing a generator and then get professional help from a licensed electrical contractor to help you safely install and use your equipment.

## *Auxiliary Solar Power*

The subject of using solar power for a whole house situation is out of the scope of this book. A quick search will provide many other books and websites devoted entirely to this subject. However, using solar power on a smaller scale for such places as outbuildings and other structures is both feasible and useful. For example; if you have a shed, outbuilding, or barn in a remote area of your property that does not have grid electrical power, a solar power system can be very useful. Additionally, having a small and portable solar power unit can be useful anywhere around your home during extended power outages if you do not have a standby generator for such emergencies. For purposes of this book section, this is a general overview of solar power systems as commonly used in rural situations.

Solar power technology is rapidly changing and it's possible to use solar on a very small scale. The basic components of a solar power system are usually the same, but the manner in which they are utilized can be easily adapted to your particular needs. Solar power systems can be grouped into two main categories, portable or fixed mounting. Before selecting a particular type, a basic understanding of how solar power works is needed.

Solar power works by converting direct sunlight into electricity. The basic components of a solar power system are the solar panel(s), a charge controller, battery, and sometimes a power inverter. The solar panel is a device that captures the sun's energy and converts it into electrical energy. A solar panel only works efficiently if it has full direct sunlight shining on the panel itself. This requires mounting the panel in an area of maximum direct sunlight during the day. In the northern hemisphere, the panel must face a due south orientation for this to be successful. Additionally the angle in which the panel is mounted should be a best compromise so that the panel receives the maximum sunlight regardless of the season and resulting sun angles to the horizon. Even clouds passing overhead on a typical day will immediately drop the power output of the panel until the cloud passes by and full sunlight resumes.

The electrical power produced by the solar panel then travels by wire to the charge controller. This electrical device performs several important functions. Primarily, it regulates the power from the panel into a useful and safe voltage that charges a battery. Other charge controller features usually include battery overcharge protection, and power cutoff from the battery to prevent damage to the solar panel during periods of darkness and at night. Finally, a battery or battery bank receives the power and stores it for use. Since batteries store DC power only, a power inverter is sometimes used to convert the DC power to a useful AC voltage when needed.

## *Portable Solar Power*

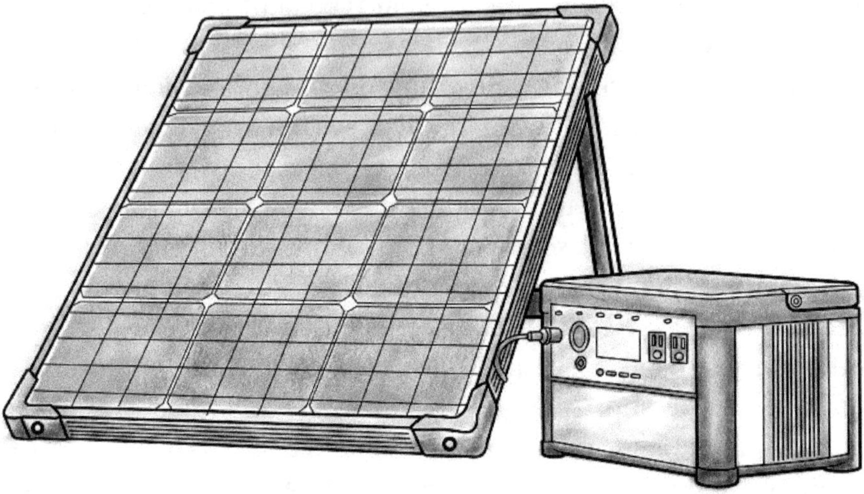

Recent improvements in solar power and battery technology has resulted in all-in-one solar power units becoming popular among homeowners. These units are small and compact. The basic components are a solar panel and the suitcase sized all-in-one solar power unit. You simply place the solar panel in a suitable location and plug your needed appliance or an extension cord into the portable power unit and you have instant electricity available. They are completely self contained and everything is automatically and safely controlled. Even homeowners who are inexperienced with solar power can be up and running in just a few minutes.

Since these units are small and have limited capacity, they are generally used for a single item at a time. They are not designed to power large appliances or complicated electrical loads. Their main use is for emergency or temporary power to a single appliance. These portable power units are available online and at home centers.

# *Small Scale Fixed Mounted Solar Systems*

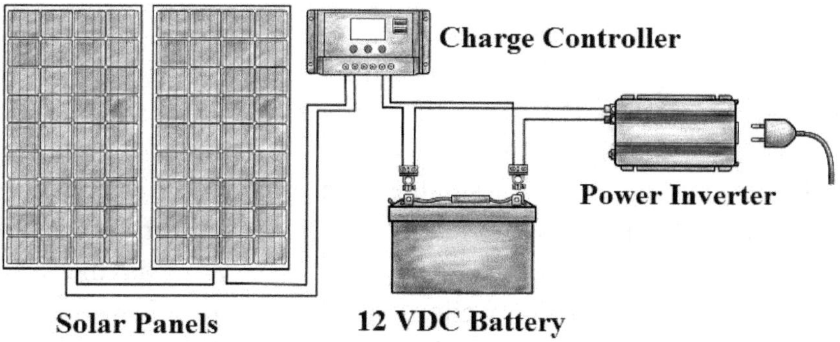


These systems are usually installed to supply power to specific place such as an outbuilding or barn for occasional use whenever electricity is needed in these locations. Because they are permanently installed, the components are separate and each should be installed and hooked up appropriately. The solar panel(s) should be permanently installed on a roof or separate mounting frame, facing the correct due south direction. Wiring is then run into the outbuilding and connected to a separate charge controller. This controller must be mounted in an area that is easily accessible for occasionally monitoring the health of the battery and the solar power system. Finally, a battery or battery bank should be installed near the charge controller.

If only DC power is needed for lighting or other minor use, then these items can be connected directly to the battery bank. If AC power is also needed, a separate power inverter unit is connected to the battery and the AC loads can be plugged into the receptacle on the power inverter.

It will become apparent that some prior knowledge of how AC and DC electric circuits work and how to calculate wattage requirements in order to properly size a solar power system, will be necessary. Again, using the readily available resources in various solar power reference books and the Internet can help you better understand how to successfully implement a small scale solar power system for your needs.

# Water and Sewer

If you have purchased a smaller rural property in a subdivision, then it is likely that you will have water and sewer infrastructure available to you. Again, the process is the same as the electric company with permits, inspections, easements, etc. If you have no municipal water or sewer available, then you will need a water well and a septic system.

You will usually own these utilities and you must pay for their installation and maintenance yourself. Water well and septic sewer systems are described in detail in a separate chapter in this book.

Typically, water wells and septic systems have become highly regulated by local and government authorities to assure health and safety. Permits may be required by the local authorities before installation. Since drilling water wells and installing septic systems can be a major undertaking, and considering the knowledge and equipment that will be needed, it is usually best if local contractors install these utilities for you.

Whatever choice you make, keep in mind that these utilities will require periodic minor maintenance, and you will need to be able to access and work around this equipment easily. For example, if you build a well house structure over your water well, take into consideration that eventually a well truck will need to pull out the well pump using a truck mounted crane for maintenance or replacement. If you have a permanent roof structure built over your well head, the roof will need to be removed and then replaced after servicing of the well is complete. If your septic system is enclosed inside a fenced yard, an access gate and clear path will be needed for a truck to occasionally pump out your septic tank. Try to think ahead and consider what will be needed in the future before you build.

# Propane

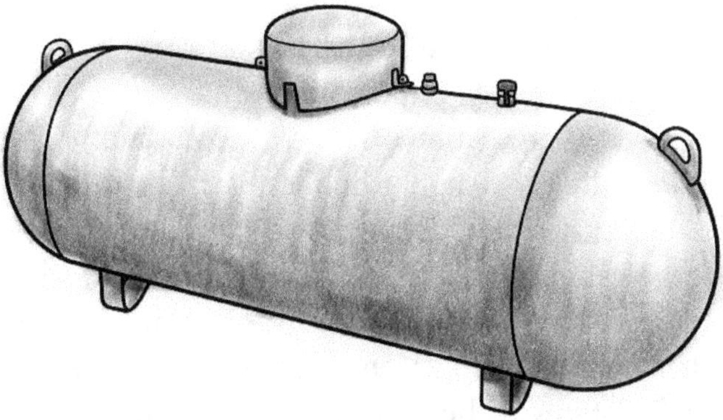

Propane gas is commonly used in rural locations. The availability of natural gas is usually reserved for city or suburban areas. Propane can be used for heating, hot water, cooking, fireplaces, pool and spa heaters, and to run standby electrical generators. Most rural locations can be serviced by local propane dealer who will bring a supply truck to your tank and refill it as necessary.

Propane tanks can either be owned by the homeowner, or more commonly, rented from a propane dealer. If you own your propane tank, you will be responsible for the periodic maintenance, inspection, and safety certification of your tank. If any of these requirements are overdue, your propane dealer may refuse to fill your tank for safety reasons. If you have a rented tank, then your propane dealer will provide these services when needed.

Propane tanks are sized according to your household usage needs. If you use propane for all of the previously mentioned tasks, a larger permanently mounted tank will be necessary to have enough reserve capacity to avoid running out of propane. On the other hand if your propane needs are very small, a portable tank may be appropriate. With this type of tank, you must physically disconnect the tank yourself and take it to the propane dealer for periodic refilling.

Permanently mounted tanks should be placed in an area of your yard that allows for easy access by the propane delivery truck. These trucks can be large and heavy, so the appropriate space to accommodate them is required. Most propane trucks usually carry a maximum of 30 feet of hoses to connect to your tank, so keep this in mind when locating your tank. If you choose to rent a tank, your propane dealer will guide you to the best area in your yard for easy truck access and set the tank in place for you.

Propane is very flammable, of course, so certain precautions must be use when installing the supply line to your house. The main supply line should be buried underground to avoid damage from lawn mowers or other vehicles. A main cutoff valve should be installed at the propane tank to quickly shut off the supply completely in the event of a leak or other emergency. Most propane supply lines are constructed of sections of black iron pipe or when longer lengths are required, a special heavy PVC hose and fittings at each end will be used.

State and local regulations concerning propane installation vary widely, so it is advised that you check with your local authorities and apply for any necessary permits before installation. Your local propane dealer will be knowledgeable about any local regulations and permitting requirements and they can usually guide you in the proper direction to start.

# Key Points...

Utilities and their easements can have a major impact on your rural property. Take the time to learn your local regulations and codes. Also discuss all of your easement options that may be available, with a utility engineer before signing an easement agreement.
Meet the utility engineer in person on your property if possible, so that you can discuss easement routes into your property.
Solar Power can easily be adapted for use for various outbuildings and other small scale applications.
If your property has no municipal water supply, a water well will need to be drilled after necessary permits are obtained.
Septic sewer systems are likely needed also and will need to be installed by a licensed contractor, after the necessary permits are obtained.
Propane is a common in rural areas. Sizing a propane tank is important as well as location.
Keep in mind that ease of access to these utilities is important for periodic maintenance by the utility companies.

# Chapter 5

# Securing Your Property

It is usually surprising to people that securing a rural property can sometimes be more complicated than for those who live in the city. Rural locations present all manner of security hazards such as trespassers, hunters and poachers, hikers, and so on… Fortunately, many electronic solutions are available to help you keep tabs on your property and animals around the clock. Of course, what may work for one area may not work at all in others, so it's best to do some research in advance, and then implement as many security features as you are able for your security and peace of mind.

Using a combination of modern security tools such as security cameras alongside standard common sense precautions such as proper signage, property boundary marking, and frequent visual property inspections, will go a long way to ensure that your property, home, and family remain safe.

## *Security Cameras*

It can be somewhat confusing to decide on a specific type of security camera to use. There are many features available on security cameras these days, and it is important to select the proper camera for it's intended purpose. For example, a WiFi camera may not be appropriate in a remote area of your property that has poor or no WiFi service at all. Likewise, a solar powered camera may be a better solution for entrance gate security where there is no electricity available.

The key to selecting a security camera is to consider exactly what basic purpose you want the camera to perform. For example, a camera that has good motion detection properties would be ideal for securing a gate or road entrance. Most of the time it would set idle, but whenever it detects motion, such as a person trying to unlock the gate, it would alert you to the potential intruder. After you have identified what specific need is the most important feature, then you can begin to research what camera model would be the best fit for that particular application.

## *Connected to the Internet or Stand-Alone?*

The first decision on selecting a security camera is whether it will be connected to your Internet or serve as a stand-alone type that records images. This can have broad implications for a rural property owner. The advantages of an Internet capable camera are nearly instant notification of an event such as movement detection and perhaps a real-time and live view coverage. The biggest disadvantage to an Internet camera is that it needs to have Internet connectivity at all times which may prove problematic in certain rural areas.

If your property spans many acres, Internet coverage may not be available at a particular location on your property that you want to monitor. A stand-alone type of camera can usually be set up and successfully function in remote locations.

The advantage of stand-alone types of cameras is that they will generally work all the time, no matter the weather or other events that may disable a typical Internet connected camera. Their biggest disadvantage is they only record what has already happened. There is no real-time notification of an event or a live view.

## *WiFi or Hardwired?*

An Internet connected camera will need access to the Internet in some fashion. This can usually be defined as a WiFi connected camera or a hardwired camera. WiFi cameras utilize wireless access to your home network to connect to the Internet. The camera stays connected to your WiFi network 24/7 and will usually send data and video to software that records events or even notify you via email or text message of an event. These cameras are very easy to install as long as you have a reliable WiFi signal at it's location and would be a good choice for an area that is too far to physically hardwire an Internet connection.

Hardwired cameras utilize an actual wire or network cable and send video and data back to another piece of hardware called a control box. These are generally used around your home and yard areas because of the close proximity to your home network which allows easy installation of the necessary cables and connections.

## *Game Cameras*

Game cameras have become very popular for security of remote areas. While they are designed primarily for taking multiple photos of wild game that are feeding in a predetermined area for hunters and animal enthusiasts, this functionality also makes them ideal for security monitoring of areas around your property such as gates and fence lines for trespassers. They are also easy to deploy and quickly move to another area as the need requires. Game cameras are now offered in several categories, including cellular phone versions, that will notify you almost immediately if it detects motion.

Many different models of game cameras are offered, and you should look at their specifications carefully to select the best model for your particular need. Nearly all modern game cameras are battery powered including some models that offer solar panel kits that will recharge the battery. Most all of the cameras are designed to have extended battery life, up to a year in many cases. They usually record photos and videos to an on-board memory device such as a SD-Card or memory stick. Because they are primarily designed for hunting enthusiasts, many are nicely camouflaged and are easily attached to a convenient tree or pole and can be well hidden from view. Nearly all game cameras have excellent night time infra-red vision capabilities.

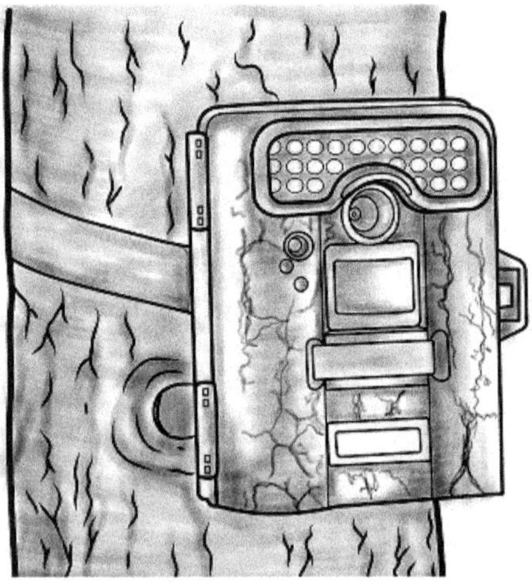

*Game Camera Mounted On Tree Trunk*

Some game camera models offer real time notification of an event via a connection to the cellular phone networks. They can send photos and videos to your cell phone nearly instantly. These types of cameras usually have a miniature phone chip installed inside and will require a cell phone signal at their mounting location. Additionally most will require some type of subscription service with a monthly charge. While most plans are very reasonable and low cost, you should carefully consider the benefits vs. the drawbacks of using a cellular camera. Nevertheless, a cellular camera can be a great security asset if an immediate notification of an event is necessary.

---

## Game Camera Placement Checklist

☑ **Mount the camera above eye level. This allows for better photo angles and discourages theft of the camera.**

☑ **Place the camera where it can properly sense movement of intruders, and not have obvious branches blowing in the wind directly in front of the camera that will trigger the sensor and cause false alarms.**

☑ **Ensure that the camera is mounted on a firm tree or other support. Smaller tree branches tend to move too much for secure mounting and will blur photos.**

☑ **Purchase an accessory SD-card reader that will work with your cell phone. This allows you to quickly check for photos from the camera while in the field, versus having to take the SD card back home to view on a computer.**

☑ **Whenever possible, point your camera to the north to avoid direct sun glare in your photos.**

---

## *Hunters and Poachers*

If you own many acres of land, hunters and poachers can present a significant and dangerous security problem. Since these intruders are almost always armed, extreme caution should be used when approaching them.

The best course of action is to notify the local law enforcement authorities to deal with these intruders. While many times a hunter may just have become lost while hunting and accidentally wandered onto your land, you can never be too cautious.

If you suspect regular activity, notify law enforcement immediately. This is another excellent reason to deploy various game cameras around your property to have a visual photo record of the trespassers.

## *Signage*

Placing posted signs or no trespassing signs around the perimeter of your property is crucial to keeping your property secure in legal terms. Most states require a landowner to place easily visible signs around their property stating that access is denied, in order to prosecute a trespasser.

Additionally, many states also allow landowners to use other methods of publicly securing their property such as purple paint marks on prominent trees along a property line.

In these cases, a special purple color paint marking is physically painted onto a tree trunk or fence post that denotes that your property line begins at that mark and entry is not allowed. This can be useful as the paint is permanent and cannot be torn down and removed like a plastic or metal sign. Regardless of what method that you choose, make sure that it is acceptable to the local or state authorities as required.

## *Illegal Drugs*

Sadly, in recent times it has become more common to find clandestine illegal drug farms set up in very remote areas to evade law enforcement. These makeshift drug farms can be quite elaborate with watering systems, generators, and camps with armed security. If you have property located near a National Forest, or some other large dense wooded area, these intruders could easily trespass onto your property and set up without you even knowing about it. Your best defense against this happening is regular inspection of all parts of your property. If your property easily shows signs of regular activity and use by the owner, most drug farmers will choose another spot as they are looking for extreme privacy and evasion from public view.

## *Gates and Entrances*

Entrance gates, as discussed in earlier chapters, need to be accessible and convenient for property owners and their guests. This can present challenges for security against entrance by trespassers. The best solution is a locked gate with easily visible no-trespassing signs to warn against entry. Other methods such as using security cameras can offer a strong deterrent against intruders. If you choose to use a security camera, try to mount it in a location that is obvious, as a visual deterrent. Additionally, mounting the camera up high and out of reach for thieves can help with the security of the camera itself.

Signs placed upon the gate entrance stating that video surveillance is in effect will also help keep a potential intruder away. For other less-used gates around your property perimeter, a chain and padlock usually works well.

## *Security Lights*

Having good outdoor lights around your home, outbuildings, and other important areas, can help deter trespassers. Many styles of outdoor lighting are available. The traditional light mounted on a power pole by your electricity provider is the most common way to light up a large area. These lights are maintained by the light company and will provide years of service.

Most other styles of outdoor lighting can be purchased online or at your local home center. Various models can be either wired directly to an available electricity source, while others use an internal battery that is recharged via a solar panel. Most of the battery powered lights are not as powerful in coverage when compared to hardwired lights. Nevertheless, these lights can still provide a useful light in areas with no nearby electricity. Many models also include a motion detection feature that turns on the light whenever nearby motion is detected. The advantage of this feature is that since the light is turned off most of the time, the battery life is greatly extended. Their biggest disadvantage is that they may not provide a sufficient visual deterrent to trespassers since they are normally turned off until they detect motion.

# Key Points...

Property security is an increasing concern for rural landowners. By using the proper and legal means to state that your property is posted and trespassers are not allowed, you can be assured that you will have the ability to properly prosecute potential trespassers.

Using common sense, and being pro-active by installing security cameras, lights, and regular inspection of all parts of your property, can help assure the safety of your family and property.

Choose the appropriate type of security camera for a particular mounting location.

Be sure to check your state and local regulations for legal signage requirements to properly prosecute trespassers if necessary.

Be aware of unusual and dangerous activity relating to clandestine illegal drug farm operations.

Install security lighting at key areas of your property.

# Section 2

# Property Enhancements and Maintenance

# Chapter 6

# Tree and Overgrowth Maintenance

If your property is located in a forested part of the country, you will occasionally need to perform tree maintenance and keep overgrowth in check. If you live in a region with dense forests or brush, sometimes you may feel like your land is trying to swallow you because the overgrowth occurs so quickly. The best way to keep this rampant overgrowth in check, is small but frequent clearing and cutting. There are various methods to clear land, but they all are intended to be followed by regular re-cutting and maintenance.

Land clearing is inevitable on rural properties, so you may as well develop a strategy to keep ahead of the growth curve on a schedule that fits best for you. Keeping a few simple guidelines in mind, tree and overgrowth maintenance can be a regular routine that can fit into your normal daily maintenance tasks.

## *Tree Maintenance*

If your property has trees, then you should assure that they are healthy. Good habits to promote good tree health include, regular pruning and trimming, keeping invasive vines away from the tree trunk, spraying for pests when needed, and preventing both compaction or erosion of the root ball. Trimming low hanging limbs should be a priority as these can become very dangerous. For example, if you are on your tractor mowing with a rotary cutter and you drive under a low hanging limb on a tree, the limb could snag your clothing and pull you off the tractor seat and backwards into the rotary cutter. Many deaths have occurred from this type of accident. One of the most important priorities in the maintenance of a healthy tree should be pruning the tree canopy and clearing away low hanging limbs.

In many regions, invasive vines can be a persistent problem for trees. Various species such as Poison Ivy, Poison Oak, Kudzu, and Honeysuckle, will quickly take over a tree trunk and canopy, causing significant harm and even killing the host tree potentially. These vines tend to lay dormant in the winter months, and when spring arrives they begin to grow and look for host structures to attach themselves to. Tree trunks are ideal for most vines, as they provide a means of reaching the needed sunlight and often provide nutrients that the vine needs to thrive. Clearing away vines on your land often means using eye and skin protection as many vines can cause severe rashes and allergic reactions for many people. For example, never burn Poison Ivy as inhaling the smoke and fumes from the burning vine can severely injure your lungs and cause eye irritation.

The quickest method to kill an invasive vine on a tree is to sever the vines near the bottom of the tree trunk. A machete knife is a great tool for this task, but extreme care must be taken to not cut into the tree bark when chopping vines. This wound on the tree trunk itself, will invite pests and diseases. After chopping the vine away from the trunk, pull the vine out of the ground and away from the tree trunk as far as possible, and then finish cutting the vine completely.

The upper portion of the vine that remains attached to the tree will soon die. Unfortunately many well established vines will take months or even years to rot completely and fall off a tree. There is not much that can be done for this, so the best advice is to trim as much of the remaining vine as high as possible so that the remaining portion of the vine in the tree will not become too unsightly as it decays.

Pests such as worms and beetles can completely defoliate a tree in the span of just a few days. This causes severe strain on the tree's health as it has to re-grow a new canopy in order to survive. Spraying the tree with a pesticide to prevent this will become a regular routine, especially if you grow fruit trees.

---

**Handy Tip...**
**It is wise to keep separate and dedicated spray tanks for different chemicals when possible. Clear labeling of each tank is important. This will help prevent the mistake of spraying a valuable plant with weed killer or other harmful pesticides because of using unmarked spray tanks.**

---

There are several methods that can be used to spray a tree. The physical size and height of the tree canopy will dictate which method is best. For smaller fruit tree varieties, a simple tank sprayer and a stepladder is all that is required to drench the low canopy with pesticide. For taller trees or mature trees that have a a very large canopy, a sprayer needs to have strong motorized pressure pump to spray straight up as high as possible to the top of the canopy.

Many of the larger tank sprayer models will have strong motorized pumps and interchangeable spray gun tips to spray a small stream a great distance. If your tank sprayer pump still cannot produce enough pressure to reach the top of a large tree, an alternate method using a standard gasoline powered pressure washer works well as a substitute. Simply mix your pesticide in your tank sprayer tank as usual, then remove the hose going from the tank to the sprayer pump and re-attach this hose to the water intake on the pressure washer pump.

This arrangement feeds the pressure washer with water mixed with pesticide from the tank. By using the smallest spray tip possible, a pressure washer can spray a jet stream of pesticide straight up nearly 100 feet. This stream will quickly drench and fog the tree canopy with pesticide and with minimal effort while you remain safely on the ground. If possible, try to stay a few feet away from the tree when spraying to avoid getting drenched with the pesticide yourself. Most pesticides can be corrosive to the metal parts of the pressure washer pump, so be sure to thoroughly wash and rinse the pressure washer pump with clean and fresh water after spraying.

Compaction around a tree's root ball is often unseen, but can become deadly for a tree over time. A tree's root ball takes up water and nutrients from the surrounding soil. The roots eventually grow and expand outward, sometimes great distances from the actual tree itself. If a tree is located in an area on your property that sees a lot of heavy foot traffic or vehicle traffic, the soil around these roots can become so compacted and tight, that the root is unable to do it's job. The tree becomes weaker over time and dies, because the soil base around the root ball has essentially turned into cement or rock. Trees located in barnyard areas can also suffer also from compaction from the constant animal foot traffic. Since this compaction often goes unnoticed till it is too late, take precautions in how you layout and plan your driveways, barnyards, and areas that will receive much foot traffic, to avoid injuring nearby trees.

Likewise, erosion near a tree's trunk can have drastic consequences on a tree's health as well. Trees tend to grow near streams, creeks, and rivers due to the ready availability of water. When these watersheds flood, they tend to wash the surrounding soil away from the roots, sometimes leaving a tree's root ball completely exposed. This is to be avoided if possible, by re-routing the stream, or otherwise taking steps to ensure that any fast moving water cannot excavate the soil under the tree. For example, large rocks can be strategically placed around a tree trunk to help deflect and slow down the water flow.

## *Clearing Overgrowth*

The understory of a forest is usually defined as all of the bushes, vines, and other smaller plants that grow under the main tree canopy. If your land has been neglected, this understory can become so dense and matted, that it is impossible to even crawl through the area. Clearing brush and overgrowth can be a challenging task physically, but the right tools and equipment can make the job considerably easier.

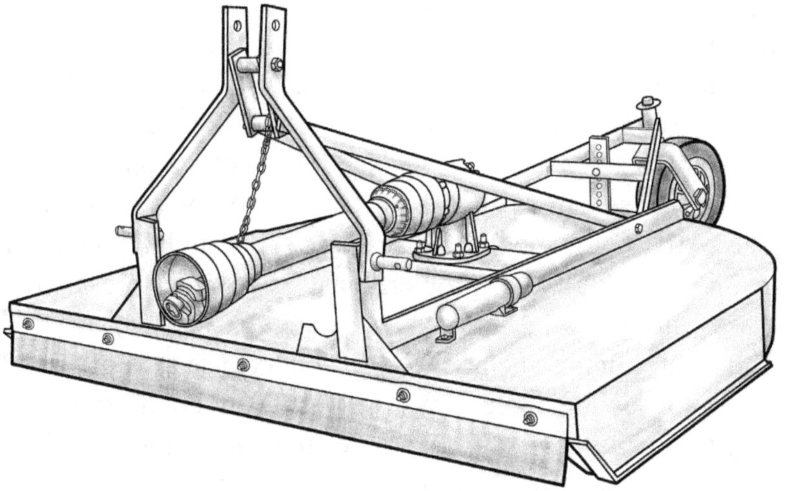

## *Rotary Cutters*

If you have a tractor already, chances are, that you also have a rotary cutter. In the South this is commonly referred to as a "Brush Hog." This term is actually a brand name that became synonymous, but the correct terminology is a "rotary cutter." These versatile implements can be used for many tasks around your property such as pasture mowing and mowing areas with dense and woody weeds. They are also able to cut fairly large sized brush and small tree sapling trunks as well.

A key point to consider is being familiar with the capabilities of your cutter and using it correctly, especially in brush chopping situations. A rotary cutter of at least 6 foot in size attached to a tractor of at least 35HP can do a fair job of clearing out a dense understory of bushes, vines, tree saplings, and general wood debris.

One advantage of using a rotary cutter is that it does a good job of clearing heavy and thick brush for the average landowner. Another significant advantage is that you probably already own the cutter as they are usually sold with the tractor as a package deal.

A disadvantage is that it is hard on your tractor and equipment, and can be a dangerous operation if you take risks and operate in an unsafe manner. Another disadvantage is that most rotary cutters will only cut down to about 4 or 5 inches in height above the ground.

When cutting heavy and woody brush, this tends to leave small and very sharp stobs of brush and saplings sticking up just above the ground and these can easily cause flat tires to your tractor and other vehicles. After a few months, these sharp stobs sticking up usually rot down and are not a major problem, just be advised to use caution in these areas until they have rotted away.

The most efficient method to clear out a dense area of brush using a rotary cutter is to nibble away the bushes in small sections before moving to another spot. For example: if you are faced with several acres of thick undergrowth, you will need to cut out a small portion of that area first, just to allow room to maneuver the tractor and rotary cutter around and under nearby trees, before you can tackle another small section.

It can be very damaging to your tractor and equipment if you try to drive over larger tree saplings while traveling in a forward direction. Because the rotary cutter is mounted behind the tractor, the tractor tends to get damaged first before the rotary cutter has a chance to cut down the saplings from the rear . Tree saplings, vines, and thick bushes, tend to snag tractor parts, and can damage the delicate exposed hydraulic hoses on the tractor.

A commonly used method is to slowly back up your tractor in a reverse direction over a section of bushes to be cleared.

This places the rotary cutter ahead of the tractor itself and allows for smoother operation by pushing the rotary cutter into the brush first before any delicate tractor parts behind it get damaged. The heavy weight of the rotary cutter will bend over the saplings and push the brush to the ground, and the cutter blades can then cut the trunks and chop the limbs. By maneuvering backwards and forward a small bit at a time, you can work your way into a section of brush and the rotary cutter will do an efficient job of chopping up the debris.

For areas that have less dense overgrowth, driving your tractor in the usual manner in a forward direction works well. A rotary cutter should have either a slip spring safety clutch or a shear pin to protect it's gearbox from major damage if it's blades encounter a solid object like a large tree stump hidden in the grass.

You should make sure that you have a ready supply of extra shear bolts if your rotary cutter uses a shear pin arrangement. Very thick and heavy cutting jobs will inevitably break a few of these bolts.

---

## Should You Go At It Alone?

**Clearing underbrush is a sometimes dangerous and arduous job that can be difficult for one person to accomplish by themselves. Before you undertake a large clearing project, take into consideration hiring a land clearing contractor to do the job for you. They usually have the proper heavy equipment that can complete the job much quicker than trying to do it by yourself. Additionally, your personal tractor and equipment will not suffer the wear and abuse that comes with heavy land clearing.**

---

## *Forestry Mulchers*

This mulching type of cutter is usually mounted on a skid steer type of tractor. These implements work by hydraulically spinning a large rotating drum equipped with many small teeth, on the front of the tractor. The drum spins at great speed, and effectively grinds up anything in it's path.

Unlike a rotary mower, a mulcher can cut through large tree trunks and will grind an entire large tree to small chips in just a few minutes. These implements tend to be very specialized and expensive, so they are mostly used by commercial land clearing contractors. Their advantages are speed and the ability to cut just about anything including trees, brush, vines and stumps. Their disadvantage is that the undergrowth tends to quickly regrow in a previously cleaned area. They cut so cleanly, that a plant may not be killed when cut and is merely trimmed to the surface. In a few months, the roots left behind can re-sprout and start growing all over again. If you have many acres to clear initially and want it done quickly, then hiring a forestry mulcher contractor would be a good choice. After your land is cleared, you will still have to maintain it regularly, using a tractor and rotary cutter.

## *Controlled Burning*

Burning underbrush is very thorough and a cost effective method also. If done correctly and at a controlled rate, the fire will not harm larger trees, and the ashes left over from the fire will help add helpful nutrients to the soil. The advantages of burning undergrowth are that there is virtually no cost involved, and the process is much less labor intensive than some of the other methods discussed previously. However, the disadvantages are significant and should be carefully considered. Burning is inherently very dangerous, and can quickly spread into devastating major forest fires. Burning is also very weather dependent, and often, when the weather is dry enough to burn properly, your local officials may have already implemented a mandatory burn ban for safety. Burning very small areas of brush is a common practice and if done carefully, with considerations for safety, can be an effective method of keeping the understory of a forest under control.

If you have any misgivings about control burning by yourself, your local fire department may be able to offer assistance or advice before you begin. Some rural fire departments may assist you with controlled burns as a practice exercise for real wildfires.

## Key Points...

The benefits of proper tree care and underbrush management are important parts of your overall property maintenance.
Make sure that you have the proper equipment available to do the job. A tractor and suitable rotary cutter along with chainsaw are the main tools needed.
If your rural property is small and you do not have a tractor, consider hiring a land clearing contractor. Likewise, if you own many acres of land, consider hiring a contractor to clear large sections of land to help prevent wear and tear of your personal equipment.
Controlled burning is effective but can be very dangerous or not legally allowed at certain dry periods.

# Chapter 7

# Rural Yards and Landscaping

When you first purchase a property, you may already have plans drawn into your mind about how you want to re-arrange your new yard and the landscaping around your home. Of course, we all want to put our individualized stamp on our home and property. One of the best things about living in a rural area is that we have total control of what our property looks like. Having no HOA restrictions, or at least very few, gives us the freedom to design our personal spaces such as yards and landscaping to our preferred tastes.

Over the time of ownership, rural yards tend to develop from newly established and elaborate landscapes often seen in fancy urban neighborhoods, to something a bit more austere and practical from a maintenance standpoint. Finding a comfortable compromise will take some time and experimentation.

Regardless of what part of the country you are located, rural yards tend to have some universal challenges that will need to be addressed. Learning how to best work with these common challenges will will allow you to develop your own individualized rural landscape.

## *Make a Plan*

Before you start building your ideal rural yard, a bit of planning ahead will help you decide the best course of action. Studying the local weather patterns in your area will greatly help in determining what to plan for. This is especially true if you are moving to an area in which you are largely unfamiliar with the local weather patterns. Almanac weather information is available through various National Weather Service websites. With a bit of research, you can look back at several years of actual data and this will help you get a better idea of what to expect in terms of typical weather impacts.

Your planning efforts should also include taking advantage of what you already have available to you on your property. Natural features such as views, lakes and streams are unmovable, so incorporating them in your landscape will be sometimes necessary. This is also true for native grasses, plants, trees, and shrubs. If your current yard area has a good stand of native grass, perhaps you should keep that, instead of digging it up to introduce a non-native species.

---

### What Happens When You Get Older?

**It is always best to consider the future when planning for your rural yard and landscaping. An often unforeseen challenge is that as we age, we may not be able to properly care for the extra maintenance needed in a overly complicated or large rural yard. You may have much additional property to care for other than just a yard, and this may take most of your time and energy away from landscaping maintenance duties. It is common to see finely crafted elaborate landscapes around a new rural home eventually become more simplified over the years, for easier maintenance.**

---

Trees are a valuable resource to provide beauty, shade, and some protection from strong prevailing wind patterns. Wildflowers, besides being beautiful, have developed natural methods to cope with the local weather patterns and can useful for providing vital food for pollinators and other wildlife. By using what is already there, you can begin to shape a successful plan for additions to your yard and landscape.

## *Driveways, Sidewalks, and Paths*

Depending on your property logistics, your driveway may be very long or perhaps just a short path to the street. Longer access roads into your property are discussed in detail in another section of this book. Shorter driveways will need many of the same considerations as longer access roads and material selection is important. Cement, asphalt, gravel, crushed rock, and other materials can be used for a typical rural driveway. Not to be overlooked, is using whatever natural material you may already have such as rocks, sand, etc.

---

**Handy Tip...**
**Asphalt may not be suitable for driveways and sidewalks in areas that get very warm in the Summer. The oils in asphalt can create a strong and unpleasant odor that will permeate through the air around your yard.**

---

In many city and suburban yards, sidewalks are purely decorative and rarely see much actual use. In a rural setting, sidewalks tend to serve a more practical purpose when compared to their city counterparts. Rural yard sidewalks typically provide daily access to remote areas in your yard as well as to nearby structures such as barns, livestock pens, etc.

In a rural yard, a sidewalk can be vital to your daily activities, therefore careful selection of materials and design will enhance your enjoyment of your property as well as it's overall beauty. Bricks, flagstone, and other hard surface materials are usually the best choice for areas that see constant foot traffic. These types of materials are the most difficult to install, but their advantage is that they last a very long time. In addition, hard surface paving materials are more resistant to weed encroachment.

---

## Do Walkways Sink?

**Yes and No. Depending on factors such as drainage and standing water, hard surface walkways can eventually sink into the soil from constant use. More likely than not, the surrounding soil and turf tends to build upwards with organic material over the years , giving the illusion that the walkway is sinking.**

---

Gravel, crushed granite, and stone dust are also widely used. Their advantages are lower cost, and easy installation. One major disadvantage of using these loose materials is that they will easily track inside your house by the small pebbles getting stuck in the soles of your shoes. These materials would be more appropriate for sidewalks around barns and outbuildings. Stepping stones can be useful for occasional access to various areas in your yard, but they are generally too awkward and uncomfortable for routine daily use. In a rural yard, weeds can be a major problem, so their control must also be considered when designing a sidewalk.

---

**Handy Tip...**
**When laying out a curved walkway or sidewalk, use a water hose laying on the ground as a movable guide to help visualize and smooth out the curves.**

---

Some rural yards utilize paths to get to areas that see infrequent use. For example, your septic system may be located as far as possible from your yard, yet it will still need to be occasionally serviced. Just keeping a clear path to this area would be acceptable, instead of constructing a more permanent sidewalk that would be rarely used otherwise.

## *Grass and Turf*

When considering what to use for grass and turf areas around a rural landscape, take a look first at what is already there. Most likely there will a mix of native grass along with weeds and other debris. Another factor to look at is the natural elevation changes in your yard as it may be uneven with natural low areas and high spots. By taking all of this into consideration first, you can then decide on what grass and turf would be best suited for your particular situation. For example, planting a non-native species such as St. Augustine grass in an area prone to drought and hot weather, may prove to be unfeasible unless a water irrigation system is installed first.

---

### Cool Season Grasses and Warm Season Grasses

**Cool season grasses thrive in northern regions. Other varieties of grasses will grow and thrive in extreme heat or drought conditions. Choose the appropriate type of grasses for your particular climate. See the Appendix for more information on various turf grass options.**

---

Another consideration when planning, is how smooth and level your yard may be. In residential developments, the ground is usually scraped to bare earth and leveled before the construction of homes can begin. In a rural yard, you may need to work with whatever is already naturally in place. For example, if your yard contains low areas that hold water during the rainy season, you will need to fill these types of areas in with topsoil and smooth them over. Look for the natural drainage patterns of rainwater in your yard as this will naturally be present, and may become an unforeseen problem.

## *Tree Stumps*

If you are carving out a yard from a previously heavily wooded area, you will have many stumps to contend with. These can be removed by stump grinding equipment that can be rented or contracted out. Regardless, after grinding, these areas will result in large circular areas in your yard that appear to be level, but in reality, they are filled with the leftover wood chips from the grinding process. Eventually these chips will decay away and a large depression will be left behind in the ground and this will look like unsightly bomb craters left in your yard and may become a dangerous tripping hazard. Although labor intensive, it is usually necessary to remove as many of the chips as possible out of the holes after grinding the stumps and fill these areas with solid topsoil that has been packed firm.

## *Handling Leftover Debris*

One of the very first decisions that become apparent to a rural property owner is where to put all of the leftover debris after cutting and cleaning your yard. Unlike a residential yard with minimal waste debris, in a rural setting this can become a significant problem. Your first thought is usually to build a burn pile someplace near the yard. While this is sometimes useful, it can present several unseen issues. For example, animals, varmints, rats, and snakes will quickly take up residence in brushy piles and can become a significant hazard around your living areas. Also, burn piles can become a fire hazard if situated too close to your home.

The best solution is to build your brush burn piles, if possible, at a farther distance away from your yard in an area that is clear from fire hazards. This will mean additional labor to move the debris, but the advantages are safety and cleanliness of your immediate yard and living areas.

## *Trash and Garbage Services*

Trash collection and disposal is necessary for a rural property just the same as those who live in the city. However rural residents have a few more options. The most common solution of course is to hire a trash collection service that serves your local area. Most rural areas have these services available. One item to consider is how far your house and trash bins are from your main entrance. If you live in a rural subdivision, this is a simple matter of rolling your trash bins down the driveway for pickup by the trash service. If your entrance gate is a farther distance from your house, then you need to devise a way to get your trash bins that further distance. Purchasing a small utility trailer is a good solution. You can keep your trash bins on your trailer and then hitch the trailer to your vehicle for your weekly transport to the front gate. This is also helpful if your trash bins tend to become overloaded and heavy.

Another solution if you do not have a trash collection service available in your area is to burn your trash. Burn barrels can be made of re-purposed steel barrels. You will need to cut or drill a few holes near the bottom of the barrel to allow rainwater to escape and to allow air inside the barrel while burning. A short piece of screen mesh placed over the top of the barrel will help deter hot ashes from escaping the barrel while burning your trash. One thing to consider is that not all household trash will burn. Items such as food cans and other debris will be left in the barrel. Eventually you will need a safe disposal area to dump out the burn barrels whenever they become full. Always make sure the fire is completely out and the barrel is cooled before trying to empty. Burning trash is not always an option during periods of extreme drought when your local county may have a burn ban enforced. Extreme caution must be used when burning any trash to avoid catastrophic wildfires.

## Choosing Vegetable Garden Areas

One of the wonderful advantages of living in a rural area is the opportunity to plant a vegetable garden.

If you are totally inexperienced with growing vegetables, you may have no idea where on your property to plant. The foremost consideration is the availability of natural sunlight. Vegetables usually need full sun in order to thrive.

Another vegetable garden requirement is water. It is likely that you will need either a dedicated water supply spigot from your water well, or a few long water hoses to be able to regularly water your vegetable plants.

Vegetable gardens tend to become fairly weedy over time and can sometimes look unsightly if placed in a prominent location in your yard. Unless you are committed to a strict routine of daily weeding and upkeep, it may be wise to place your vegetable garden in less prominent area around your property.

## Storing Firewood

You may use firewood for heat or simply the enjoyment of a fire in a fireplace. Either way, you will want a supply of cut firewood that has been stacked properly and kept dry. If you use firewood as your main source of heating, then you will naturally need a much larger quantity of wood versus the casual fireplace user. If this is the case, placement of your wood storage will become a major concern and careful planning will save much future effort.

Firewood generally has to be cut, split, and dried properly in order to safely use. Burning freshly-cut green wood will build up a creosote coating in chimney flues and become a significant chimney fire safety hazard. Depending on your location, drying times for firewood can range from a few months to several years. Your firewood will need a shelter such as a shed or some other covering to prevent rain and snow from slowing the drying process even further.

You should locate your firewood stacks near enough to your home for convenient access, yet far enough away so that they are not unsightly or present safety hazards. A clear sidewalk or path to your woodpile is advisable for use in wet weather or snow.

*Dry Firewood Storage Shed*

## *Swimming Pools*

Yes, even rural homes sometimes have swimming pools and spas! If your pool is located in an area that has a lot of ground animals such as snakes, rats, rabbits, and such, they will naturally be drawn to the area and try to drink water out of your pool. They sometimes fall in the water and drown as they are unable to crawl over the ledge of the pool to get out. While it is sometimes unavoidable, you can mitigate these issues to some extent. Keep shrubs and ground cover plants away from the immediate pool area. It's a good idea to install a floating safety ramp to allow animals that do fall in the water to safely get out. This is a good safety precaution for your pets also.

Lastly, an above ground pool will be far less likely to entice animal hazards because the tall steel walls of the pool above ground level present a natural barrier to animals versus an in-ground pool located right at ground level.

## *Wildlife Issues*

In a rural location, you will likely have wildlife problems from time to time. Large wildlife such as feral hogs, bears, and aggressive deer can become a significant safety hazard.

Smaller animals such as skunks, raccoons, armadillos, and possums, can become a nuisance and can destroy your lawn plants quickly. Your best option is to build a perimeter fence of the appropriate type, to keep these unwanted visitors outside of your yard. It may not always work successfully, but a good fence will keep the majority of wildlife out, and keep your children and pets safe.

# *Wildfire Dangers*

Fire danger has become an increasing threat in recent times. Weather related events, overcrowding and over population, and poor land management practices has increased the danger of wildfires dramatically in many locations. No matter if your property is heavily forested, or in the middle of a grassy prairie, you need to make a wildfire plan. This plan should include mitigating any obvious wildfire hazards around your property.

Typically, these hazards include having heavily underbrushed forests too close to your home. Other hazards include having trash and debris near your yard, and not cutting fire lanes to prevent wildfires from quickly traversing your property. Take a few moments to look around your yard area and try to remove easily combustible materials.

Another important item in a wildfire plan is access for fire trucks. Fire trucks and their equipment tend to get a bit larger each year and their bulk, and enormous weight can create challenges for quick access inside your property. For example, your entrance gate may be too narrow to allow the fire truck to get inside your property, or your entrance road to your home may be too soft or mushy to withstand the weight of a heavy fire truck.

Plan ahead for these challenges, and do your best to make sure your that your home is easily accessible to fire trucks and equipment.

---

**Handy Tip...**

**If you are unsure if your road or driveway has the necessary space to accommodate a fire truck, ask your local fire department if they can pay a visit with their largest truck and check for any problems in advance, before a real emergency.**

---

# Key Points...

Planning ahead is key to designing a suitable rural yard and landscape. Take into account future maintenance as we age.
Using natural grass and flowers may be a better choice when compared to introducing non-native species. Try using a mix of both for versatility. When landscaping, consider the natural drainage and slope of your yard to prevent unforeseen standing rainwater problems.
Locate walkways and various paths in your yard thoughtfully and consider using the proper materials in their construction.
Consider a solution for proper and safe garbage and trash disposal.
Carefully plan your firewood storage location and have a dry walkway built for frequent use in the winter. Make sure your firewood is properly seasoned and aged before burning.
Install a floating safety ramp in an in-ground swimming pool to allow thirsty wildlife and pets a means to escape if they fall in the pool.
Mitigate wildfire dangers and place brushy burn piles in a distant location. Always consider fire truck access onto your property for safety.

# Chapter 8

# Water Wells and Septic Systems

Water wells and septic systems are commonplace in most rural landscapes. Because these are important mechanical systems for your home and property, you should have a good understanding of their principles and how they work. Both water wells and septic systems can be expensive, thus regular maintenance and upkeep is necessary to protect your investment. Additionally, water wells and septic systems are usually regulated by local, state, and sometimes federal authorities, so printed records and periodic inspections will likely be required. Most states have strict licensing requirements for water well and septic installers. Because these systems require specialized heavy equipment, it is necessary to hire commercial contractors to install septic systems and dig water wells. Installing these systems is not a DIY project usually.

# Water Wells

A modern water well consists of a deep drilled hole in the ground that is lined with a protective pipe called a casing. Casings are commonly constructed of a special PVC pipe that is pushed inside the freshly drilled well hole in the ground. The casing keeps the hole from collapsing in on itself and filling in the well. Additionally, the casing is used to form a sanitary seal around the bore hole at the ground surface to prevent water contamination from surface groundwater which may contain fertilizer runoff and other nearby hazards.

Most modern wells obtain water near the bottom of the well from a natural aquifer deep below the ground surface. The bottom few sections of casing are usually perforated to contain many small holes and a fine mesh screen which allows water from the aquifer to fill up inside the casing, while excluding sand and mineral particles.

A submersible pump or a jet pipe is then lowered into the casing below this water level, to pump the water out of the well and into a tank at the surface. Many well configurations have been used in the past, but most modern wells use either a jet pump or a submersible pump to retrieve water from the bottom of the well and pump it to the surface.

## *Water Well Pumps*

A jet pump is used mainly on shallow depth water wells. If your property is located near an aquifer that is relatively shallow to the surface, a jet pump can pump the water from this aquifer using suction, much like a drinking straw. There can be many variables in deciding if a jet pump is suitable for your well. Your water well drilling contractor will guide you with the best selection for your particular location.

A submersible pump is located at the bottom of the well and is underwater at all times. Unlike a jet pump that sucks water, this well pump pushes water to the surface using an interior pipe inside the casing. The advantage of a submersible pump is that it can be used at very deep depths. Many land areas commonly have water wells that are over 350 ft. deep, and a good submersible pump can pump water to the surface from these deep depths.

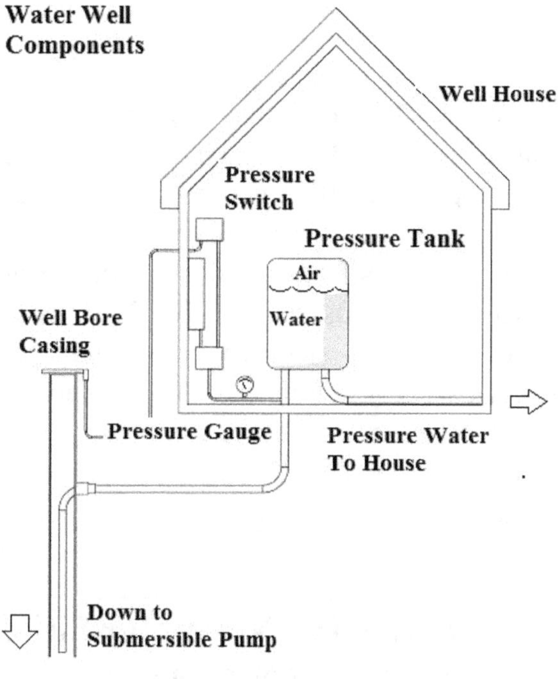


*Basic Water Well Parts Diagram*

# *Pressure Tank*

Once the water is pumped to the surface, it must be collected and stored at a sufficient water pressure to provide adequate water flow to your house plumbing. A well pressure tank stores the water it receives from the well pump. The tank is sized in volume to create a reserve quantity of water, so that you can use water without triggering the pump on and off erratically each time you open a faucet. This helps preserve the lifespan of the water pump. Additionally, as water is pumped into the tank, water pressure is increased to a predetermined point at which the pump is automatically turned off. The pressure tank maintains this pressure until you open a faucet, and slowly the pressure drops enough to turn the pump back on and the tank fill process starts over again.

## *Switches and Electrical*

A pressure activated switch assembly is located between the well pump and the pressure tank. The switch has the simple purpose of turning the well pump on or off, depending upon the pressure inside the pressure tank. This switch is manually adjustable, so that both the high and low pressures can be adjusted for a particular installation.

Most modern well pumps require 220 VAC and the pressure switch will have the necessary electrical connections for this voltage. Extreme caution must be used whenever you service or adjust a pressure switch. The electrical connections can be fatal if accidentally touched or shorted. Additionally, if too much pressure is allowed to build up inside a pressure tank, it can rupture and cause severe injuries.

---

### No Electricity - No Water Either

**If you experience frequent power outages and you are on a water well system, you can expect to be without water also. Not much of a problem for short periods, but this can be a major problem for extended outages. A backup generator would be a good idea. Since most well pumps operate on 220VAC, make sure that the generator that you choose can provide that power. Additionally, if you are purchasing a generator for emergency use only, you may only have enough capacity to operate your well pump by itself only. Always consider the usable wattage output of the generator vs. the maximum wattage consumed by your appliances. If necessary, a separate generator plug can be installed at your well pump for quick temporary use.**

---

## *Basic Water Well Maintenance Tips*

For the most part, a good water well installation will be trouble free for many years and will require only minor ongoing maintenance. Occasionally, excess air can build up inside a pressure tank. This will displace most of the water inside the tank with air and cause water faucets to spit out air whenever they are opened. Depending on your tank configuration, a method to bleed off this excess air is built into the tank itself, so check for air bleeding instructions usually provided by your drilling contractor. Another frequent problem is the exact opposite. The tank will become completely waterlogged with no air inside at all. A small amount of air is needed inside the tank to create the water pressure. If the tank only contains water, the pump will cut on and off very rapidly which can cause damage to the pump. Again, instructions provided with your pressure tank will explain how to drain off a bit of the water and introduce the proper amount of air inside a tank.

Most well tanks have a pressure gauge to indicate the water pressure inside the tank. This is needed to monitor proper well operation. The gauges tend to fog over in the direct sunlight making them unreadable, or sometimes water can seep inside the gauge itself and damage the internal parts of the gauge. Replacement gauges, along with many other well system components, are readily available at farm and feed stores. A pressure gauge is easily replaced by shutting off the well electrical power supply, draining all of the water out of the tank and relieving the water pressure, and then simply unscrew the gauge and screw in the replacement.

Likewise, replacing a pressure switch is accomplished in the same manner. Be sure to pay close attention to the proper electrical connections. If in doubt, a licensed electrician can make the necessary connections for you. Finally, be sure to keep the area around your well head and pressure tank clean and mowed to assure proper operation. Ants, in particular, have a tendency to build nests and beds inside the electrical components of a water well and cause shorting and a fire hazard.

# Septic Systems

A septic system is required in most rural areas, and is usually regulated by the local authorities to assure public health and safety. In its most basic form, a septic system converts harmful sewer water and fecal matter into benign effluent discharge water that is safe for the surrounding area. This effluent water is either distributed just under the ground surface and absorbed back into the soil, or is sprayed into the air much like a water sprinkler. Most modern septic systems consists of two main varieties. A conventional septic system has at least one septic tank and a network of shallow field lines buried just below the surface. The sewer waste is treated by naturally occurring anaerobic bacteria that convert the waste inside the septic tank into effluent discharge water which is then drained by a network of underground field pipes.

An aerobic system also uses a septic tank, but it has an additional aerobic tank, and a holding tank for effluent discharge. An electrical pump in this holding tank then discharges the effluent to the surface using a sprinkler system. An air pump constantly pumps air into the aerobic tank, and this creates naturally occurring aerobic bacteria which treats the sewer waste. This type of system has the advantage of quicker sewer waste treatment using aerobic bacteria vs. the use of anaerobic bacteria in a conventional septic system.

## *Conventional Septic Systems*

Conventional septic systems have been successfully used for many years. Their biggest advantage is that there are no moving parts and no electrical power is required. The field lines are carefully installed slightly downhill from the septic tank, and gravity causes the effluent to trickle into the field lines by gravity and to be slowly absorbed into the surrounding soil. As more sewer water is flushed into the septic tank, the same amount of treated effluent is discharged into the field lines to drain away.

Their biggest disadvantage is that the field lines tend to get clogged over time and the septic tank eventually overflows and discharges raw sewer onto the ground. Tree roots and other plant roots especially love to grow around and inside the field lines and this can create blockages and leaks at the surface.

Another disadvantage is that a conventional septic system takes time to convert the sewer into safe effluent, and may not be able to keep up with the sewer discharge from a large household. If you have a high septic flow rate it can become too easy to over run a conventional septic system and flood the septic tank and field lines causing a mess in the yard.

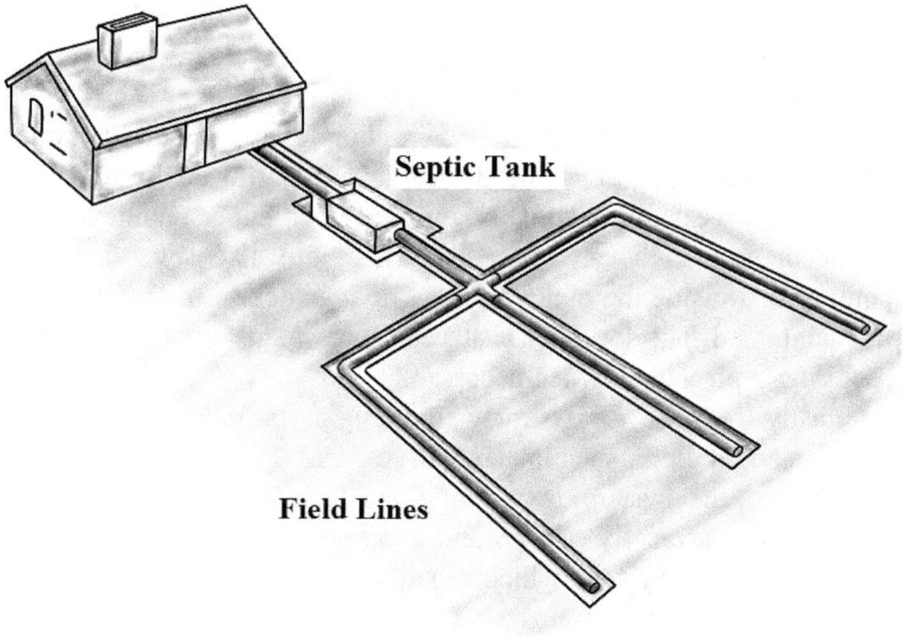


*Conventional Septic System*
*Layout*

## *Aerobic Septic Systems*

Most states and counties now require any new septic systems that are installed to be an aerobic system. As stated earlier, using aerobic bacteria to treat sewer waste is more efficient and quicker and can easily keep up with the sewer treatment demands of a large household.

Aerobic septic systems have both advantages and disadvantages, however. Their biggest advantage is that they do a good job of treating sewer waste and the effluent is usually cleaner when compared to a conventional system. Because there are no field lines necessary, they are more suitable for small property yards and other more enclosed lots. The sprinkler heads can be easily adjusted to a suitable spray pattern to discharge the effluent away from nearby structures, houses, gardens, etc.

Their biggest disadvantage is their complexity. An aerobic system needs electrical power at the discharge pump and at the air pump. These parts wear out eventually and will need either maintenance or replacement, which can be costly. There are also several moving components inside the tanks, such as float switches, that will need to be maintained. The sprinkler heads can be damaged by a lawn mower, requiring replacement when necessary.

Lastly, because of the many moving parts, most states require frequent periodic inspection by an official licensed inspector, to assure that the system is working as designed. These inspection contracts can typically cost around $250 yearly, and will be required for the life of the system, which can add up to a substantial amount.

Aerobic septic systems can vary in design and complexity between different models and how big of a system is need for a particular application. Some models use simple chlorine disinfection tablets, while others may use a liquid chlorine injection system. The air injection pumps are usually either a diaphragm type of pump or a rotary style pump. The control box contains all of the necessary electronic control boards and connections from the float switches.

The basic operation of an aerobic system is straightforward; Sewer water from the house flows by gravity to the first septic tank. Heavy solids settle out and fall to the bottom of the tank and are digested by anaerobic bacteria, much like a conventional septic system. As the tank fills up to the top with effluent water, it overflows into a second tank where air bubbles are introduced into the effluent. This supports colonies of aerobic bacteria which further digests the effluent.

Eventually this effluent water flows into a holding tank. Here, a small amount of chlorine is introduced into the effluent to kill off any left-over bacteria and to disinfect the effluent water. This holding tank eventually fills up with effluent to the point that a float switch inside the tank activates an electric pump. This electric pump pushes the effluent water out to a series of water pipes and sprinkler heads. The effluent water is sprayed into the yard on the surface to eventually evaporate.

**Aerobic Septic System**

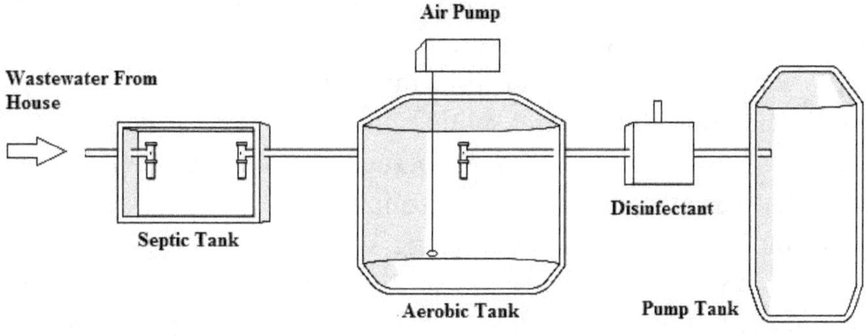


# *Septic System Maintenance Tips*

Regardless of which system that you use, a few precautions will go a long way to prevent costly repairs. Your first line of defense is to be careful what you flush down the toilet.

Various towelettes and hygiene products are commonly marketed, but many are not septic safe as they do not biodegrade. Common items such as paper towels and table napkins can take a surprisingly long time to dissolve inside a septic tank. Of course, avoid flushing any discarded medical waste or prescription or over-the-counter drugs as these can quickly kill off the bacteria living inside the septic tank and cause foul odors and other problems. Be cautious when flushing any chlorine products such as some toilet bowl cleaners for the same reasons.

If you have an aerobic system and the malfunction alarm located in the control box suddenly sounds, check to see that the holding tank with the pump is not clogged or overflowing. Another reason for an alarm may be that the air pump has stopped working. Rebuild kits for most air pumps are available online as are new replacement air pumps.

If the submersible effluent pump has failed, a call to a service company will probably be required as these are more complicated to replace properly.

Both types of systems may need periodic pump-outs of the septic tank by a septic tank contractor. This is a good practice anyway to keep your septic system from becoming clogged up and allows for better solids digestion in the septic tank. This process involves using a large vacuum truck and hoses to suck out any non-biodegradable debris that has settled in the main septic tank.

If you have a conventional septic system with buried field lines, pay attention to nearby trees and shrubs as their roots will eventually grow towards the pipes. Never plant any woody plants on top of a field line area. If you observe constant wet patches on the surface, a call to a service company may be needed to unclog the field line.

Most states and jurisdictions require ongoing inspection reports pertaining to the condition and operation of an aerobic septic system. A licensed inspector will physically inspect your aerobic system every few months. They will be looking for proper operation of the air pumps, control box and discharge pumps.

Additionally they will test for chlorine residual in the pump-out holding tank, and test or the effluent PH balance.

Most inspectors will file a condition report with the proper authorities, after inspection. Septic inspection companies usually charge a yearly fee to inspect your system on the required schedule.

Alternatively, some states allow the homeowner to inspect their own system and file their own reports, if they have taken a wastewater course and obtained the necessary licenses and certifications. Depending on your area's license requirements, you may wish to simply hire an inspection company for this task.

---

## What Happens If I Kill Off The Bacteria?

**The colony of bacteria that lives in your septic tank is crucial for it's operation. These beneficial bacteria consume the waste and convert it into benign effluent water that can be safely disposed. But what happens if you accidentally spill a bottle of toilet bowl cleaner into the toilet?**

**Most gel type of toilet bowl cleaners contain chlorine as their disinfecting agent. This chlorine will also kill all of the good bacteria colonies living inside your septic tank. Your tank will go rancid and start to smell.**

**Fortunately nature starts to rebuild the beneficial bacteria colonies as soon as possible and then the process starts working again. How quickly your tank becomes back into balance again depends on how much chlorine was spilled. This may take anywhere from 24 hrs to several days, or even longer in some cases.**

**The best advice is to be careful about which cleaning products that you use, and be careful about what products you flush such as towelettes and other toiletries.**

---

# Key Points...

Clean freshwater and safe sewer treatment are paramount to your family's health and safety. Both water well and septic systems tend to be complicated and costly, so regular maintenance and inspection will be needed. By understanding the basics of how each of these systems work, you can better maintain these systems yourself and diagnose most common problems that occur.

Water well pumps usually fall into two categories; submersible or jet-pump. Pressure tanks store the pressurized water for supply to the house plumbing.

Water well pumps will not work in the event of a power outage. Consider using a standby generator to power your well pump in an emergency.

Septic systems usually fall into two categories; conventional or aerobic. Most areas now require aerobic systems to be installed in new builds. Periodic maintenance, and pump-outs are necessary in either type of system.

Aerobic systems will need to be inspected on a regular schedule by a licensed inspector.

# Chapter 9
# Property Outbuildings

Rural outbuildings can be defined as barns, sheds, storage buildings, and other smaller structures around your property. One of the benefits of living in a rural area is that you usually have free choice in the design and construction of these structures. Permits may still be required, and local and regional building codes may still be enforced, but in most cases, outbuilding design is up to your personal preference.

The main design considerations to consider are how you plan to use your outbuilding and your personal style preference for it's appearance. Sometimes the intended use of these structures will be the deciding factor in it's design with no real regard to appearance. This can be perfectly acceptable if your outbuilding is located on a part of your land not easily seen by the public. For larger structures such as barns and metal buildings, take more careful consideration of it's design in order to blend in naturally with the overall style of your home and property.

For example, a traditional wooden hay barn with a hay loft and cupola may look out of place located right next to a sleek and modern style home design. Your property and building style will reflect your own personal taste, and outbuildings should at the very least, try to be constructed in a similar manner and style, when possible. In most cases, outbuildings are usually constructed out of convenience or a specific need, and as such, they tend to be simply designed for that purpose. Interior design and layout can be as simple or elaborate as you prefer, or simply have no interior at all. The choice is up to you.

## *Pre-Manufactured Outbuildings*

Building supply houses and home centers offer a myriad of pre-manufactured outbuildings in many styles and designs. If you are uncomfortable or inexperienced in carpentry, these types of buildings offer a quick and easy solution for your needs. One advantage is having a nearly instant building delivered to your location and ready for use immediately. Another advantage, is that you can purchase a building that is more elaborate than anything that you would typically attempt to build yourself.

The biggest disadvantage of pre-manufactured buildings is they tend to range from being very well constructed, to very low quality, and it is sometimes hard for the average homeowner to distinguish the difference in quality.

Lower priced pre-manufactured buildings are usually constructed of substandard materials and while they look good initially when new, they may not hold up over time. Their advantage is that they are usually cheaper to purchase, which may be an important factor in your decision. You need to study each type of building carefully, and look at the warranty for exclusions before making a decision on which building to purchase.

Many building manufacturers offer very well constructed buildings from both wood and steel and sell them through local independent dealers in most rural areas. After you place an order, the completed building is delivered to your property and set up and leveled to the ground. These companies tend to offer higher quality buildings and have better warranties.

An important consideration when purchasing a pre-manufactured buildings of any type, is how you will be able to have it delivered inside your property. Even smaller outbuilding designs can seem large, when they are on top of the bed a delivery truck that's trying to navigate your small driveway or entrance road. Narrow gates, low overhanging limbs, steep hillsides, and wet areas, are all significant obstacles, and these must be considered when selecting a location for your building to be delivered. Your building dealer or manufacturer will usually make a pre-delivery visit to your location to look for these problems in advance and help you make the appropriate decisions for access to your property.

*Pre-Manufactured Building*

## *Build It Yourself*

You may choose to build your own outbuildings using plans from the Internet, or perhaps just using your own ideas to serve a specific purpose. For example, simple three-sided shed plans and other examples can easily be found on the Internet and adapted to your own dimensions.

Most sheds can be constructed using standard lumberyard wood and metal siding and roofing. For longevity, consider using ground-contact rated treated wood for the framework.

## Locating A Suitable Spot

☑ Since a building structure is meant to be permanent, you need to choose a suitable long-term location. Consider the purpose of the building and how you intend to use it. For example; if you just need a simple outbuilding to store yard tools and a lawn mower, find a location that has easy access to your yard for convenience. On the other hand if you need a building to store hay and feed, then the best location would be nearby your animals or livestock. Also try to avoid awkward situations where the location of your outbuilding or shed looks out of place and unsightly around your home if possible.

☑ If your outbuilding will need utilities such as electricity, water, and sewer connections, then take into account the necessary steps to bring in these utilities. Locations that have utilities nearby would be favorable compared to locating an outbuilding far way from any established utility connections.

☑ If your land needs to be cleared of trees and brushy overgrowth to accommodate your outbuilding, take care to ensure that the area that you select to build is suitable with regards to drainage, slope, and is reasonably level. Often overgrown areas will conceal issues such as water drainage that will later become a problem during construction.

☑ If your outbuilding location is in a remote or unused area of your property, a suitable access road will be needed first in order to bring materials to the building area. If this is the case, it is advisable to complete the roadway first to avoid damaging your property during construction.

## *Before You Build*

If your outbuilding design is relatively small, it is advisable to purchase most of the larger building materials in advance of construction. This will ensure that all of your materials such as wood siding or roofing materials are all consistent and will avoid the problems of having supply availability issues during the middle of construction. By having all of your main building materials on-site before construction begins, your building will be completed in a timely manner, instead of waiting on out of stock supplies.

Make sure that your building location is clean, dry, level, and compacted as much as possible to avoid working around obstructions. For example, remove any brushy stumps, rocks, or other debris where the building is to be located. Likewise, make sure to take any necessary precautions to protect any nearby trees and other valuable plants to prevent damage while building.

Lastly, when laying out the position of your building in relation to the surrounding area, take into account unforeseen problems such as morning or evening sun glare, prevalent wind direction (especially during hard winter cold fronts) and consider how square in position you want your building to be in relation to other nearby structures.

# *Metal Roofing and Siding*

Metal roofing, or "tin" roofing as it is commonly called, is arguably the most common material used in the construction of outbuildings these days. There are many reasons, but the main advantages are low cost, ease of use, and durability.

The drawbacks of metal roofing are that it can get dented and damaged during hail storms or if an overhanging tree limb falls on it. Also, the style of a metal building may not reflect the tradition of other structures located in your local area and may look out of place. Nevertheless, metal roofing and siding should be considered if it is appropriate for your circumstance.

Regardless of style, most metal roofing comes in standard sheets of 3ft. wide in coverage, and lengths of 8ft, 12ft, and 16ft are commonly available at building supply stores. R-panel tin is usually flat in appearance with metal ridges formed along the length to add rigidity to the sheet.

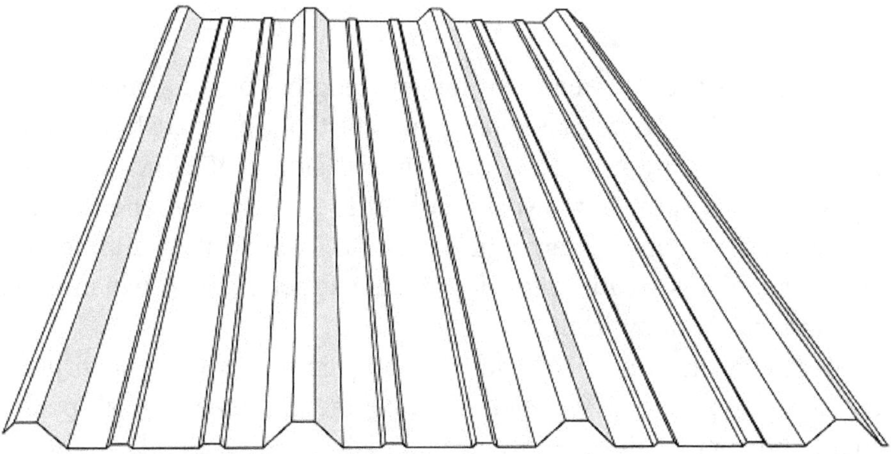

*R-Panel Tin Sheet*

Standard corrugated barn tin is usually wavy in appearance with the ridges along the length curved in a u-shape. Both styles can be used for either roofing or siding as the need requires.

*Barn Tin Sheet*

If your structure requires longer lengths of tin, most metal building supply houses can supply and cut the longer custom lengths to order specifications. Metal roofing and siding of either type will require a supporting framework under it to serve as the anchor point for the tin sheets and to carry the structural loads of the building. The tin serves only as weatherproofing for the structure, as it has minimal structural strength by itself.

Working with tin is easy for the average homeowner with just a few simple tools and supplies. Cutting the tin sheets to a specific length and shape can be easily accomplished with a standard circular saw fitted with a special metal cutting blade. Eye, face and ear, and hand protection is required when cutting, as small bits of steel will be ejected in all directions when using an electric saw. Marking lines for cutting can be more easily seen if made with a permanent marker.

Special sheet metal screws are used for attaching the tin sheets. These screws utilize a socket style screw head and have a metal cap plate with a rubber washer under the cap plate. When the screw is driven through the sheet of tin, the cap plate compresses the rubber washer and makes the hole weatherproof.

Sheet metal roofing screws generally come in two different types, with each serving a specific purpose. Self-drilling screws have a small drill bit formed on the end of the screw so that it will drill a starter hole before screwing two sheets together. For example, if two sheets overlap each other, you will need to drill through both the upper and lower sheets in the overlap area simultaneously, in order to screw the sheets tightly together.

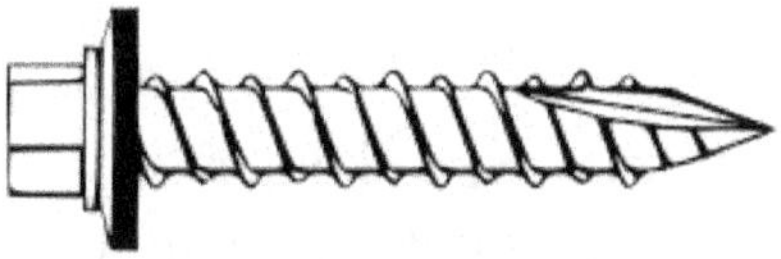

*Standard Pointed Sheet Metal Screw*

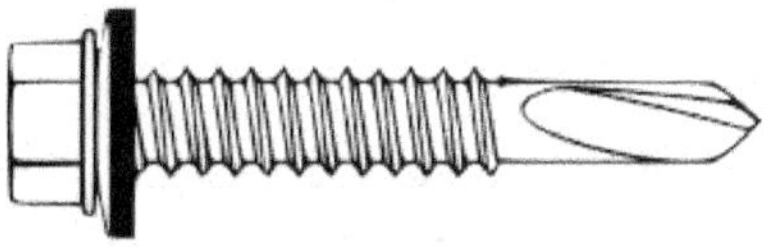

*Self-Drilling Sheet Metal Screw*

The other type of sheet metal screw has a sharp point on the end and is usually a bit longer in length so that it will screw through a single sheet and grab tightly into the wood behind the tin. These types of screws are intended to secure the tin sheets to the underlying wood framework. A battery-powered screw gun makes the job of attaching tin sheets using either type of sheet metal roofing screw quick and relatively easy.

It pays to take the time to match the color and style of other buildings on your property. This gives your property an overall unified appearance. Metal siding and roofing can easily be painted using ordinary latex house paint to match the style and color of other buildings on your property.

It can look somewhat untidy to have several outbuildings that are near each other that are all painted totally different.

Lastly, when landscaping around outbuildings, try to keep plantings, hardscapes, and other features in the same style as your general yard area for ease of maintenance.

---

**Handy Tip**

**If you need to snap a chalk line across several sheets of tin for a long cut, use blue colored chalk, as it will eventually wash away with rain, while a red colored chalk tends to be more permanent, waterproof, and unsightly.**

---

# Key Points...

Outbuildings are necessary to store tools, tractors, and other equipment, and keep them out of the weather. Animals sometimes require outbuildings also to protect them or to contain them.

Outbuildings are an integral part of rural living in the country, and if properly designed and constructed, they can add to the value and appearance of your property. By taking the time to carefully consider your requirements, and selecting the best design to meet these requirements, you can be assured that the outbuilding that you choose will be a useful addition to your property.

If you choose to build your outbuilding yourself, carefully consider it's placement on your property for it's intended use.

Metal tin is commonly available in two different styles - standard and R-panel tin.

Use the correct sheet metal screws for their intended application.

Paint your outbuildings around your property in a matching color and style for a unified appearance.

# Chapter 10

# Tools and Equipment

Specific tools will be needed for proper yard and property maintenance in a rural setting. For example; because of the rural nature of your property, overgrowth of weeds, vines, and bushes are more prevalent. Weeds will need to be controlled and bushes and vines cut back or removed. It is vital to have the proper tools to tame these persistent invaders. The following is a list of the most basic tools needed. More specialized tools are discussed in other sections of this book.

What tools are really needed and what is not needed? This is a very subjective question as everyone's situation will be different. Some tools can be purchased as they are needed, thus saving on initial expenses when you are first starting out maintaining your property. Equipment and tool manufacturers are always marketing their latest and more powerful tools, but the reality is that you can get by very well with just these basic tools listed in this chapter.

It is likely that your list for needed tools will also include some that have not been listed here. Everyone who lives in a rural setting will quickly learn what tools they will need to complete the task at hand.

## Yard Maintenance Tools

### *Shovels*

There are two types of basic hand shovels, each serving a specific purpose. While each type of shovel will work for either purpose in a pinch, having the proper shovel specifically suited for the job will make the work much more efficient and easier to accomplish. A round nose shovel or digging spade is designed to easily cut into soil to dig a hole or trench in the ground. Some are shaped in the familiar wide and curved blade style with a rounded cutting face while others are very narrow and long to facilitate digging a narrow ditch or trench.

The other type of shovel is designed with a flat and wide face to move loose material and soil around. This type of shovel often has a square face that helps when scooping material out, especially in corners. It can also be used to shave off and level the surface of the soil. This shovel is a poor candidate for digging holes because the flat edge makes it very difficult to push into the soil. When shoveling loose material such as compost, gravel, and mulch, a flat faced shovel will move more material faster than a standard round nose shovel.

Lastly, shovels of either type will have various handle styles. Usually digging shovels such as a round nose, will have a long straight handle. This allows you to easily manipulate the shovel while digging a deep hole and to assist in prying or using the handle as a lever against stubborn rocks or roots. Trenching shovels are usually for shallow holes and thus they are often equipped with a shorter handle and a D-style grip for easier handling while tossing soil out of ditches etc. Handle types are largely a matter of personal preference and comfort. If possible, try to purchase tools such as shovels locally so that you can get a true sense for how the tool feels in your hand prior to purchase.

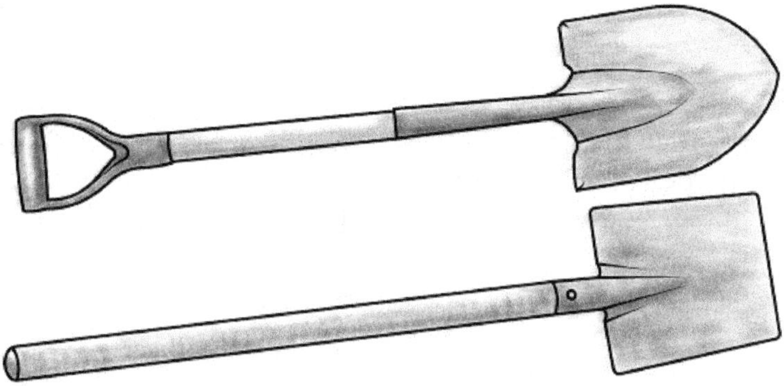

*Round And Flat Nosed Shovels*

Modern shovels use a variety of materials to construct the handles. Wooden handles for shovels have been around for centuries and are easier on your hands and palms. Their chief drawback is that a wooden handle will rot easily if not properly cared for and stored out of the weather. Most wooden handles are constructed of either hickory or ash wood. Good maintenance includes brushing a coat of boiled linseed oil on the wooden parts each season, and keeping the handles wiped free of mud and debris. Of course, storing them indoors or under a shed is vital to preserving the wood and prolonging their lifespan. One thing to note with wood handles is to store them upside down and hanging from the shovel head or body. This is to prevent warping of the handle over time and to allow moisture to drain away from the handle socket, thus preventing the common rotting issues often seen in this area.

The other type of handle material often used in modern shovel construction are fiberglass handles. These types of handles often include a rubber grip of some type and tend to be a bit stronger than their wooden counterparts. One important thing to consider when storing a shovel with a fiberglass handle is to keep it out of direct sunlight. The UV rays from the sun can cause rapid deterioration of the fiberglass and weaken the handle.

## *Rakes*

A standard leaf rake is a necessity for cleaning leaves and yard debris. A garden rake with short stiff tines is nice to have for raking out dirt clumps and removing weeds, but is not absolutely necessary.

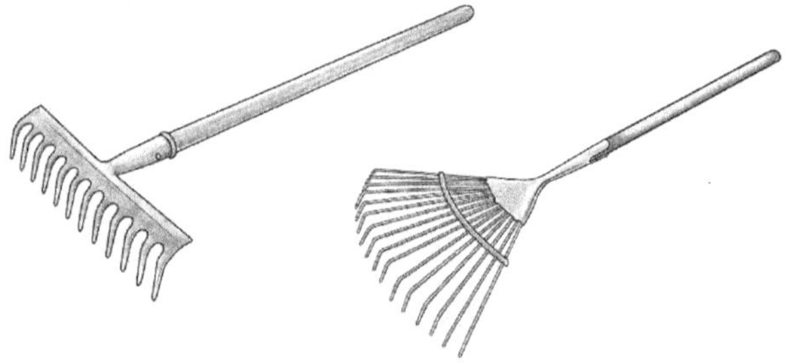

*Garden Rake* *Leaf Rake*

## *Pruners and Loppers*

Pruning shears will be needed for keeping shrubs and plants from being overgrown. Loppers are different from pruning shears in that they have a sturdier handle. They also have short and stout jaws that can cut much larger limbs up to around 1" in diameter. While the two tools do similar jobs, both tools are necessary for the proper pruning of the natural overgrowth. It is imperative that you keep vines and small trees from overgrowing by regular cutting and pruning. In the southern regions of the country, vines will quickly overtake a tree trunk and grow as high as the tree canopy which is not only unsightly, but can be harmful to the trees that they attach themselves to.

## *Wood Axe and Hatchet*

The difference between an axe and a hatchet is the length of the handle, usually. Also a wood axe will usually have a double cutting head while a hatchet will usually have a single head.

Both will be useful for chopping limbs and debris from trees and bushes that are overgrown. Caution must be used while using these tools to avoid injury. Both of the tools can glance sideways off the wood that you are cutting if not handled correctly, and injure the user or bystanders.

## *Wagon or Yard Cart*

Once you have chopped up your overgrowth and it's on the ground, you will need a way to remove the debris to a suitable disposal area or burn pile. A heavy duty hand pull wagon or yard cart can be a real work saver. When selecting a yard cart, look for one that that has a tilt dump for the bed. This is useful for dumping dirt and compost or mulch and saves the extra work to shovel it out. Additionally, the pull handle should be able to attach to a lawn tractor in some fashion for pulling heavier loads longer distances. Most wagons or yard cart handles can be temporarily tied to a hitch ball on a lawn tractor by using a small piece of rope.

*Yard Cart With Folding Sides*

## *Wheelbarrow*

A wheelbarrow is the tool of choice for moving dirt, compost, and mulch. It is also very handy for mixing cement and mortar. Various models and styles of wheelbarrows are available. Some models have two wheels while some have one wheel. Likewise, some have metal handles and some have wood. It's all a personal choice as to which type feels the most comfortable for you. The models with larger diameter wheels will be much easier to navigate over dips and lumps on the ground versus a smaller wheel.

By far the biggest problems that occur with wheelbarrows are the tires. They nearly all seem to be flat when you need them the most. This problem can be avoided by using a proper size inner tube instead of a tubeless style of tire. Periodically checking the tire pressure will help also. The best solution but the most expensive is to replace a leaky and wobbly tire and wheel with a no-flat solid rubber tire and wheel. These can be readily purchased at farm stores and tool outlet stores.

---

**Handy Tip...**
**Always purchase a wheelbarrow or yard cart with large and wide wheels. This will allow for easier pulling by hand when moving heavy loads.**

---

Some wheelbarrows are made with a plastic tub while others will have a stamped steel tub. Either of the options will usually suffice for most general homeowner needs. An exception is if you plan on mixing a lot of cement or mortar in your wheelbarrow, a heavy metal tub will the better choice. Always store a wheelbarrow out of the rain and weather if possible to avoid rotting the handles or rusting of the steel components. If you must store it outside, make an effort to store it in an upright position to avoid rainwater from collecting inside the tub.

# Power Tools

Power tools for yard maintenance are the backbone of any rural homeowner tool arsenal. These can be further classified into two major types: battery powered and gasoline powered. Commonly, property owners will need a assortment of both types as some jobs require the extra power that a gasoline engine provides, on the other hand, battery operated tools are far more convenient for many situations.

## *Pruning Chainsaw*

A small electric battery powered chainsaw that can be hand held or mounted onto a telescoping pole is important to have for pruning overhanging limbs from trees. These limbs can be especially dangerous if you get tangled in one while mowing with a lawn tractor or garden tractor. A pruning saw will be able to reach up around 10 feet to trim off the limbs while you stay safely on the ground. Caution! Never use a chainsaw of any type while standing on a ladder as this can be extremely dangerous.

---

**Handy Tip...**
**Keeping a sharp chain will make your work faster, easier, and safer. There is a wealth of information on-line about properly sharpening chainsaw blades. Many styles of chain sharpeners are available to help you maintain a proper angle while hand sharpening.**

---

## *String Trimmer*

These tools can be either battery operated or gas powered. Both have advantages and disadvantages. A battery powered string trimmer is a handy grab-and-go tool that is always ready for a quick trim of weeds.

It is cleaner, lighter, and easier to use. A good quality name brand battery powered string trimmer has nearly the same power as a gas powered version. As with any battery powered tool, try to keep a spare battery or two (or three!) available so that you can quickly switch out dead batteries for uninterrupted use.

A gas powered string trimmer can be a real convenience and is almost necessary when working around your property if you are far away from your house. As long as you have the proper mix of two-cycle gas/oil mix in a fuel can, you can work uninterrupted for hours which is not possible with a battery operated tool.

## *Leaf Blowers*

Again, the battery powered vs. gas powered discussion. A battery powered leaf blower is really the only practical way to sweep clean decks, sidewalks, and patios. A broom will get the job done too, but at a dreadfully slow pace when compared to a blower. Battery units are always ready and available to work at a moments notice such as before guests arrive for a garden party or similar touch up situations. A gas powered leaf blower really shines when it's yard clean up day and you have larger areas to clean that a battery powered unit will not have the power to be able to accomplish. If your rural yard contains many trees over several acres, a backpack type of gas leaf blower will work like nothing else.

## *Push mower*

A reliable gasoline powered self-propelled push mower is necessary for yard maintenance. While an electric push mower will work fine for small yards, most rural homes have much larger areas to mow than a typical city lot. A gas powered mower will have more power available to cut rough grass and small sticks that are usually prevalent in rural yards.

In fact, most rural yards have widely varying types of grass with everything from St. Augustine to native Bermuda, to just plain native weeds that will be needing mowing and trimming regularly. Side discharging or mulching mowers are the norm in these types of situations as baggers will quickly and inconveniently fill with dirt and sticks too often.

## *Riding Lawn Mower*

These mowers can usually be classified into two main types - tractor style and zero turn radius styles. There are also other designs such as stand up riders with sulky carts and compact riders, but these are usually not suitable for most rural acreage and yard situations. Gasoline powered riders are currently the most suitable mowers as electric riders have not been developed enough to be seriously considered for extensive rural landscapes yet.

Tractor style mowers resemble a small tractor and usually have a belly mounted mower. Some of the larger units also have various attachments such as snowplow blades which may be very desirable if you have a long driveway to plow in the winter. The main advantage of tractor style mowers versus the zero turn models is power. Tractor style mowers generally start at around 15HP with increases up to nearly 35 HP and can have significant pulling power and traction. Horsepower is a primary consideration when selecting a rider for your particular situation. If you have a lot of heavy weeds, overgrowth, uneven ground, deep ditches, and need a snowplow in the winter - then a tractor style mower is your best choice. Additionally you can tow a small trailer for landscaping projects when needed. If by chance you do not own a full sized garden tractor, then a small tractor style lawn mower can be a substitute with the right accessories. While a full size garden tractor is far more versatile, a small tractor style lawn mower can do a fair amount of work, especially in tight areas.

When shopping for a tractor style mower, there are many different items to consider. Engine brands and styles should be considered. Most of the larger tractor style mowers will have a two-cylinder engine which is smoother, quieter, and generally more reliable. Of course more horsepower also can mean more fuel consumption, so keep that in mind, too.

The next main item to consider is transmission types, the choices usually being either geared transmissions or hydrostatic drive transmissions. Geared transmissions are generally stronger in terms of overall tractor pulling power. They usually have a stick shift and a clutch pedal and take a bit of time to get used to operating. Hydrostatic transmissions are hydraulically powered, usually by a belt connected to the engine. There is no gear shift or clutch pedal. There is simply a forward and reverse function usually combined into a single foot pedal. You push forward on the pedal for increasing speeds and reverse the pedal to go into reverse. Taking your foot off the pedal causes the tractor to stop motion and stand still. Hydrostatic transmissions will spoil you with their simple ease of use, and are much easier to drive for young people and smaller framed people. The biggest disadvantage of hydrostatic transmissions is maintenance of the transmission itself is usually not possible, as most models are sealed units from the factory. If your hydrostatic transmission goes bad, you'll have to buy a complete new transmission unit which can be expensive. The other major disadvantage is that hydrostatic transmissions are not designed to pull heavier loads. You can easily overheat and damage a hydrostatic transmission when pulling a loaded and heavy landscape trailer.

Lastly when shopping for a tractor style mower, consider the wheel sizes - especially the rear wheels. Larger rear wheels can really be an advantage if your property has a lot of ditches, ruts, and uneven terrain. Larger wheels help keep your tractor more stable and give you better traction while driving over these obstacles,which is a huge safety advantage. You can purchase different tires with various tread patterns to suit your grass and terrain, if needed.

---

## Lawn Mowers And Riding Lawn Mowers New Or Used?

**The more expensive items such as lawn mowers and gas powered equipment can be purchased previously used at significant savings over a brand new model. People tend to discard equipment when it doesn't work perfectly and buy new again. Most of the times the problem is easily repairable but they do not know how to repair it and just prefer to buy a newer model. If you are handy at diagnosing and repairing things you can often get mowers for next to nothing or even free in some cases. Folks who live in the country are resourceful and smart. If you see the need for a new tool or new equipment for an upcoming project, look around and consider all of your purchase options well in advance so you can "work smarter and not harder."**

---

Zero turn radius (ZTR) mowers have gained in popularity over the years and are the favored type used by professional landscape companies. Their biggest advantage is speed. The can easily mow a circle right around a post or tree trunk without reversing. They are extremely maneuverable and great to use if you have many tight spots, trees, or obstacles to mow around in your yard. Most consumer-grade ZTR mowers have engines in the 20 HP to 25 HP range. They are generally all configured about the same with a belly mower, a driver seat in the middle, a rear-mounted engine, and two large levers to control the mower direction. Driving one becomes very intuitive with just a few minutes of practice. Their biggest disadvantage is that most ZTR mowers are designed for just one thing and that is mowing. They are nearly impossible to use for other handy tasks such as towing trailers, snow plowing, and garden dirt work. They also sit low to the ground and will become stuck very easily in wet terrain or ditches. Even with larger rear wheels, they just cannot match the versatility of a tractor style mower.

If your yard has a lot of obstacles, trees, and smooth terrain with domestic grass, then a ZTR would be a great choice.

The final decision on which style of mower to purchase is the one that has the most versatility for your situation. If you already own a full size garden tractor to use for general tasks around your property and you just want to quickly and easily mow your yard with the least effort, then a ZTR would perhaps be your best choice. On the other hand, if you need a tractor to pull landscape trailers, plow snow in the winter, and have a fairly rough, wild, and uneven yard, then a tractor style mower would suit you better because of it's ability to do many different tasks.

## Property Maintenance Tools

While many of your yard tools can also be used around other areas of your property, there are a few other tools that are handy to have for general rural property maintenance.

### *Sprayers*

A tank style sprayer that has an electric pump can be very helpful when killing unwanted weeds and overgrowth. The small one gallon handheld pump type of sprayer is not suitable for the coverage needed in larger areas and long fences. A tank sprayer will generally hold from around 10 gallons up to 50 gallons of chemicals and has both hand held spray nozzles and rack mounted bar nozzles. The hand held nozzle gun is used most often to spot spray weeds and to spray fence lines and such. A bar mounted spray is best used for killing wide swaths of weeds while being pulled behind a tractor or ATV.

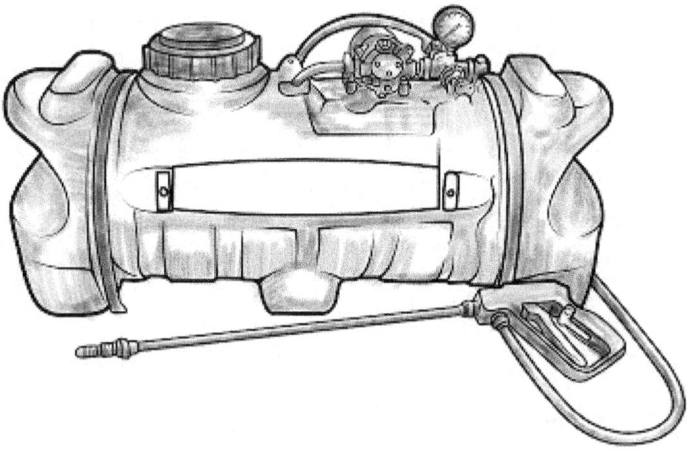

*15 Gallon Electric*
*12-Volt Tank Sprayer*

Tank sprayers generally come with a polyethylene tank that is somewhat transparent so that you can quickly see at a glance the tank chemical levels inside. They also have a small electric pump motor that is powered by 12 VDC such as from your lawn mower or ATV battery. Some of the very largest tank sprayers have a pump that is mounted on the PTO shaft of a full sized garden tractor which allows them to develop high pressure to spray great distances.

Sprayers for home and rural use generally come in three different configurations. One type has a 15 gallon tank and a small pump motor mounted directly on top of the tank. They are completely self-contained except for the battery and have a small hand held spray gun for chemical application.

These units are very light and can be easily moved around and stored when empty. They are easy to strap on the rear equipment rack of an ATV for convenience. The second type of sprayer is usually a bit larger and is permanently mounted on a rolling cart or trailer. These can easily be towed behind a small lawn tractor to the far areas of your property.

The larger variety of sprayers have a more powerful electric pump. They also have a mounting arrangement for a 3 foot wide bar sprayer to cover wide swaths of ground while being towed. The third type of sprayer has a large tank of at least 50 gallons and is mounted onto a sturdy and large steel frame that is designed to attach to the 3-point hitch on a full sized tractor. They generally have a PTO powered pump and thus need no 12 VDC electric power. These types of sprayers are designed to use very large booms of nearly 30 feet in length and can spray very wide swaths in large fields and pastures.

---

**Handy Tip...**
**Adding a few drops of dish detergent into the tank of your sprayer will allow the chemicals to more evenly coat the leaves of plants and retard evaporation in the sun.**

---

Regardless of the types of sprayers that you use, there are some basic maintenance and cleaning directions that need to be followed. Most weed killing or fertilizer chemicals are highly corrosive to certain metals and can rust out nearby metal objects or machinery very quickly. Immediately after use, the sprayer must be completely cleaned out by rinsing with clean water and wiped down. The pumps are especially susceptible to damage and corrosion from chemicals. Any electrical connections will corrode extremely quickly if not wiped clean of spray chemicals. Most sprayers are already designed for easy and quick cleaning with removable hoses, spray guns, and easy-to-service pumps. If you are using a spray boom, be sure to flush clean water through the nozzles to avoid clogging the tiny spray holes.

## *Pressure Washer*

Pressure washer design has really become refined in recent years. These units are invaluable for maintaining and cleaning tools and equipment. In a rural property setting, items such as mowers, tools, and vehicles can quickly become muddy, dusty, full of grass clippings, and such. A pressure washer makes for a quick and easy clean-up. Keeping your equipment clean should always be a priority for longevity and ease of maintenance. Residential types of sprayers usually fall into the following two categories.

Electric pressure washers are generally smaller, easier to use, and more convenient for a quick spray down of your equipment. The advantage of being small and light makes them easy to store away when not in use and they don't require gasoline or oil. Their biggest disadvantage is they do not have the PSI spraying force of their gasoline counterparts. Another consideration is these must be plugged into an electrical outlet for power and thus you cannot take them to a distant barn or shed for use unless you already have electricity installed there. Finally, electric power washers are usually lightly built and have few serviceable components so they are basically non-repairable.

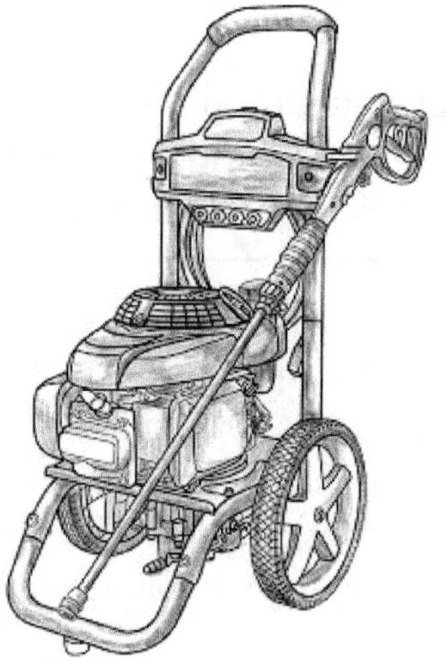

*Gasoline Powered Pressure Washer*

Gasoline powered pressure washers are best suited for heavy cleaning jobs. They can be used in any area as long as you have either a long water hose or a separate water tank that can be refilled as necessary. Their biggest disadvantage is they need gasoline, oil, and require regular maintenance like any other engine powered equipment. Gasoline powered pressure washers generally come mounted in a steel frame with small wheels for mobility. Some models have the water pumps mounted vertically under the engine and some are horizontally mounted. Either version works well. The pumps are usually serviceable and replaceable when necessary. You can also purchase extra hose sections if you need the longer length. For example, when spraying the side of a building while up on a ladder, etc.

Either type of pressure washer will usually have accommodations for removable spray tips and accessories. For all around general cleaning and washing, a turbo nozzle is a good choice. This nozzle has a small rotating pin inside that increases the spraying force while protecting the surface that you are spraying. For example, if you use a standard fixed-nozzle on a wooden deck, you will risk damaging the wood surface by splintering and digging tracks into the wood surface.

---

**Handy Tip...**
**Protect and prolong your pump's service life by using a special lubricant. These "pump saver" lubricants can be found online or at most stores that sell pressure washers and supplies.**

---

A turbo nozzle will avoid these hazards when used properly. Turbo nozzles are a good all-purpose choice when used for cleaning wood and steel painted surfaces on equipment.

For cleaning cement slabs and driveways, a special-purpose rotating bar nozzle will cover a larger spray surface to save time and allow for even surface cleaning without leaving streaks in the cement.

## *Water Hoses*

If you own even a small rural property, you are inevitably going to need several water hoses. They are indispensable for reaching the far areas of your property. If they are of sufficient size, you can easily connect several water hoses to cover distances of several hundred of feet. They key is to get a larger diameter hose if you plan on using them to cover long distances.

Water hoses come in many different sizes and are constructed of a myriad of materials. The main thing to consider when selecting and purchasing a water hose is how you plan on using it and how much weight you are willing to tolerate while using it. A larger hose will be much heavier and bulkier. This is a very important but often overlooked consideration. Another feature to consider is the material that is used in it's construction. Some hoses are made of a woven vinyl while other are a heavy duty rubber compound. If you plan to drag your hoses over cement or rocky ground, a heavy rubber hose would be a better choice. The last major item to consider are the end fittings. Solid brass machined fittings are hands-down the best choice, but they can be expensive. Unfortunately, many of the cheaper imported hoses have shiny brass plated fittings that are in reality a cheap zinc material that looks good initially, but these inferior fittings quickly corrode and seize, creating a lot of frustration. Always try to keep your hoses coiled neatly and stored out of the direct sun, as the harmful UV rays will cause them to deteriorate quickly and become stiff and brittle.

# Key Points...

Hand tools are the backbone of any rural property tool collection. If possible, try to purchase hand tools locally to see how they feel and operate.

Powered tools such as lawn mowers, chainsaws, and pressure washers are appropriate for major jobs such as heavy cleaning and mowing.

New or used equipment such as mowers should be a personal choice considered carefully.

General property maintenance tools should be carefully selected for the jobs anticipated and maintained regularly.

# Section 3

# The Logistics of Country Living

# Chapter 11

## Service People and Deliveries

Living in a remote or rural area can present some unique challenges when it comes to accommodating service people and visitors to your property. Folks who live in the city have become accustomed to receiving daily deliveries and packages. Services of convenience such as grocery deliveries, restaurant meal deliveries and easy availability to transportation services have become so commonplace in urban environments that they are now taken for granted as part of routine daily life.

In certain rural areas, some of these services are available on a limited basis. It is undeniably convenient to take advantage of these services if they happen to be offered where you live, but successfully using them requires a bit of planning ahead. For example, you may live in a rural area only a few miles from the nearest town, yet if you have a locked entrance gate to your property, the delivery services will not be able to complete their delivery.

By thinking in advance about what services you may need, you can work proactively around any inconveniences. You may have to become a bit creative in your solutions, but here are some tips that will help you.

## *Rural Package Delivery*

The popularity of Internet commerce has made it commonplace to order many items online, thus package delivery has become an issue for folks who live in a rural location. Nearly all of the major online retailers and delivery companies will deliver packages to even very remote locations. The challenges that occur however, are actually receiving the package after it has been delivered to your address. For example, if your home is not visible from your entrance gate, or if your gate is shut or locked, the delivery service will either just leave your package on the ground next to your gate or return the package to the vendor. If your package is left unsecured and laying on the ground, it may be a tempting target for thieves, and additionally, weather such as rain or snow may damage your package. Leaving your gate opened for a delivery service may not be an option if you have livestock, and many delivery service policies will not allow driving onto a rural property if there are obvious obstacles such as a poorly maintained entrance road.

A good solution for securing most common package deliveries is to construct a drop box or parcel locker at your entrance gate. The delivery person can then leave the package inside the locker and it is protected from potential thieves and inclimate weather. The majority of package deliveries tend to be in small to medium sized boxes, so a locker should be large enough to be able to accommodate most package sizes. As for security, if thieves are common in your area, you can leave an opened padlock inside the locker with plainly written instructions for the delivery driver to lock the dropbox after the delivery is made. Be aware that this may not always be successful, as many drivers will miss or ignore your instructions and leave the dropbox unlocked anyway.

One other drawback to this method, is that any other additional deliveries that same day will be left unsecured because the dropbox is now locked any other delivery services will not be able to use it. Nevertheless, this is usually a good workaround to deter most package thieves or weather concerns.

A parcel locker or dropbox can easily be constructed of exterior grade plywood with a couple of hinges for the lid, and a locking hasp. It should be mounted near your entrance gate in an easily seen location for the delivery driver and clearly marked as a package locker intended for deliveries.

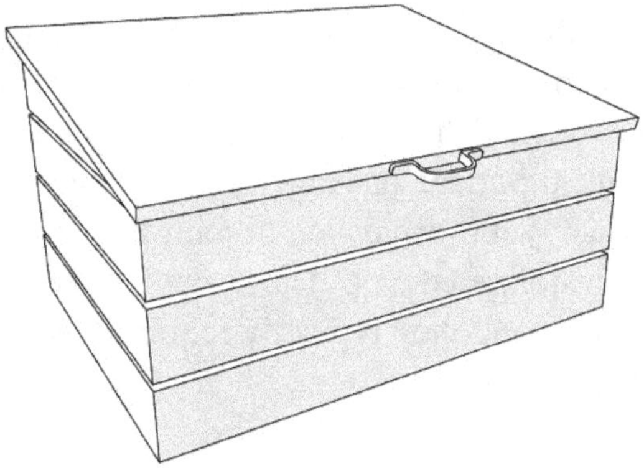

*Delivery Drop Box*

An often unexpected situation with lockers and dropboxes is that insects such as ants or wood spiders tend to make nests inside the locker. They may even crawl inside your cardboard packages occasionally. This can be remedied by regular spraying of a pesticide inside your parcel locker to deter insects and rodents.

Rural mail service is also commonly available in most locations so using a mailbox that is sized large enough for small packages is advisable. Having your address clearly marked for both mail and package deliveries will eliminate confusion for delivery drivers who may be unfamiliar with your area.

---

**Handy Tip...**
**Leave a note inside your mailbox for the postal worker to leave any over sized packages in your delivery locker instead of the mailbox. Some postal locations may have strict rules against the worker leaving their vehicle, but most will usually try to accommodate your request if your parcel locker is located nearby the mailbox.**

---

Finally, a handy if not a somewhat high-tech solution for security is available for mail and package locker security. There are electronic devices available that you can attach to your mailbox and parcel locker that will send you a text message on your cell phone whenever the door or lid is opened. This is very convenient if you are waiting for delivery of an important package, and will save on unnecessary trips up and down your driveway or entrance road to see if the package has been delivered yet. These devices usually work via a small internal battery and they typically require a WiFi signal in order to connect to your cell phone.

## *Service People*

While you may take pride in doing much of the maintenance around your property yourself, it will be inevitable that you will still need to employ service people from time to time. These folks will need access onto your property, and you will need to work out a way to let them in. The simplest solution is to meet them at an agreed upon time, and open the gate and manually let them in. This may be important to do also if you live a long distance from your gate as they may become lost after driving into your property if the road to your home is not clearly marked.

You can also program a temporary entrance code into your keypad if your gate has an electric gate opener installed. This will allow them limited time access to your property. This option is handy if you are unable to meet them in person.

A lower tech solution is to leave a key in a designated but discreet area around your gate with instructions for the service person to leave the key in the same spot on their way out. Your experience with any regular service people such as lawn services, etc. will dictate which method would work the best for your particular situation.

## *Visitors*

One of the joys of living in a rural location is having friends and family visit and enjoy your beautiful property with you. Many of the same issues concerning property access for service people also pertain to visitors. Usually, meeting your visitors in person at the gate to let them onto your property is the best and most welcoming solution. This may not always be practical in all situations however, and so arrangements must be made in advance for letting them inside.

If you are planning an event such as a party with multiple guests, the best solution is to open your gate and leave it open for the duration of the party, if possible. If you have livestock, it will be necessary to temporarily secure them elsewhere so that they don't wander off of your property. If you live on a large acreage property, temporary signs for visitors pointing out a clear path to your home is always a good idea, so that folks don't get lost and end up at your barn instead of your home. Lastly, it is very important to make sure that your entrance road is maintained and smooth enough for the average car to safely pass.

# Key Points...

Try to make final delivery of your packages, or entrance onto your property for service people or visitors, as easy and convenient as possible for them. Making their job easier is always a good practice, and especially so if your location presents unique challenges. Many deliveries are performed by the same people each time, and establishing a regular and convenient delivery routine for them will ease the frustration of having missing packages or missing service people when you need them the most.

Purchase or build a suitable parcel locker or dropbox for reliable package delivery.

Leave a note for your Postal worker to leave oversize packages in your parcel locker, if possible.

Electronic mailbox or dropbox alarms are useful to determine if a delivery has been completed, instead of making multiple trips to check on deliveries.

If you are hosting a party or other event for visitors, temporary signs to lead them to your home may be a good idea if your entrance road is long and your property is large.

# CHAPTER 12

## Setting Up A Rural Home Office

Foremost on the mind of many folks is the ability to work from home in a rural environment. Setting up a suitable home office in the country presents a few challenges. Internet access is problematic in many rural locations and having the ability to easily use your cell phone can be hit or miss. Nevertheless, there are a few steps that you can take to help mitigate some of these difficulties. Simply asking other people in your local area what they use for cellular access and Internet connections may provide a good starting point. With these recommendations in mind, you can explore all of your options for connecting to the outside world and setting up a viable home office.

In spite of the potential technical challenges, you can enjoy the peace and solitude that country life naturally brings, while still being able to stay in touch with your colleagues, and getting your work done.

# Cell Phone Reception

A common problem for folks living in a remote or rural area is adequate cell phone reception. Fortunately, the issue has improved dramatically in the past few years. Because cell phones have largely replaced traditional land lines, their importance as a vital infrastructure has been prioritized. Thus cell phone providers have increased their efforts to build more towers in more rural areas. Additionally, new technology is constantly improving the efficiency of cellular reception.

Despite these improvements, you may find yourself in the unfortunate situation of still having spotty reception, or worse yet, no reception at all. There are several steps that you can take yourself to improve your phone reception. Cell phone amplifiers and external antennas, as well as suitable building practices, all help to some extent.

## *Amplifiers and External Antennas*

Using an amplifier to increase the cellular signal inside your home or home office can be very effective. Their disadvantage is that you must have some cell phone reception outside, even if only marginal. They work on the principal of taking a small and weak signal from outside and amplifying it and then re-broadcasting it inside your home at a greater strength. Basically working as a radio repeater, these units will not work successfully if they cannot receive an outside signal to begin with.

Amplifiers usually employ a highly efficient and directional outside antenna. When installing the antenna, you want to first aim it in the direction of your nearest cell phone tower. These antennas are much more sensitive than the standard antenna built inside your phone. By having this antenna mounted outside, you usually eliminate the possibility of signal interference created from obstructions inside your home.

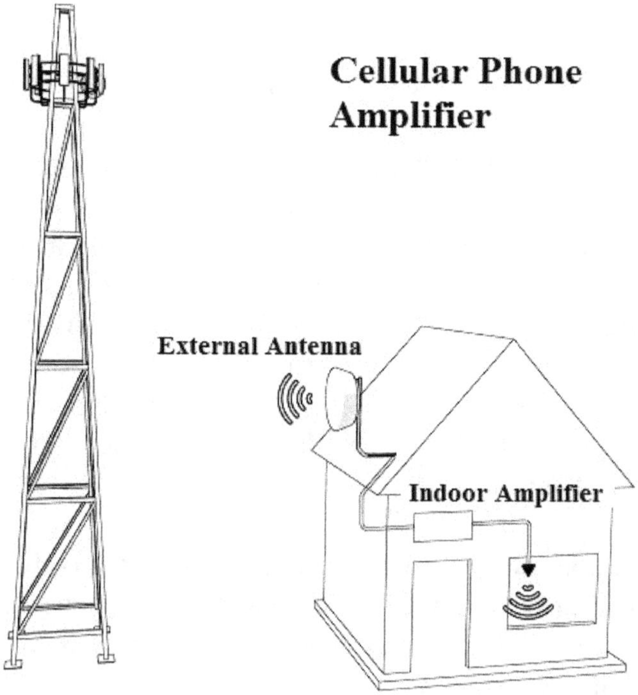


*Cellular Phone Amplifier Layout*

Metal roofs and metal siding should not affect your reception if the antenna is mounted properly outside of these obstacles. Mounting an external antenna is fairly easy. Most antennas are mounted on a pole or mast. Additionally, you can also choose to mount an external antenna directly on a wall or other flat surface.

---

**Handy Tip...**

**There are several Internet websites that provide up to date maps showing cell phone tower locations. They usually provide coordinates to your home location, and you can use these coordinates and a hand compass to help you align your external antenna to point exactly towards the closest tower.**

---

## Cellular Amplifier Mounting Checklist

☑ Keep the overall distance from the outside antenna to the indoor amplifier as short as possible. The cabling to connect the antenna to the amplifier inside your home should also be kept as short as possible. Longer lengths tend to degrade the already weak signal coming from outside. Most amplifier kits provide a pre-made cable to connect the amplifier to the antenna. You may have to work with this fixed length by using a compromise of the best location for the inside amplifier versus the best location for the outside antenna.

☑ Make sure that there are no immediate obstacles directly in front of the antenna, such as buildings, walls, large tree trunks etc. The closer the obstacle is, the greater it will degrade reception of the antenna.

☑ Make sure the cabling from the antenna to the inside amplifier is secure. You can use plastic zip ties, electrical staples, and electrical tape to secure the cable and to prevent it flopping around in the wind, thus greatly prolonging the life of the cable.

☑ Whenever possible, choose the highest installation location possible to mount the antenna. The higher that you mount your external antenna, the better it will perform.

☑ Be aware that items such as electric fence controllers and solar panel inverters can sometimes cause interference issues.

The indoor amplifier will either have an internal antenna or some units may use an external indoor antenna. These re-broadcast the signal inside your home, so they should be mounted in a centralized location if possible. Again, if you are working with a fixed length antenna cable, you may have to experiment a bit, to find a suitable location to mount these items. The amplifier will also need a source of electrical power from a wall socket inside your home.

Once you have properly located and mounted all of this equipment, power on the unit, and in a few moments you should notice better reception on your phone's display. Experimentation seems to be the key to success with these units. To find the most efficient places to mount both the external antenna and the indoor amplifier, you may want to temporarily set it up at various locations around your home to try it out before making a permanent installation.

## *Telephone Landlines*

Yes, believe it or not, many traditional phone companies still provide landline service to rural areas. This can be especially important if your cell phone reception is spotty or difficult at your location. Many folks who live in rural areas still use a landline phone for everyday use. Some advantages are the ability to call out in any weather, and having a clear traditional phone call without signal dropouts and lost connections. The disadvantages are mainly logistical.

If your home is located a far distance from the main road where most landline cables are located, it may be expensive to run a private phone line into your property. Also, if you own the landline telephone cable that is located on your property, you may be responsible for it's upkeep and maintenance. If a tree falls on your phone line, you will need to make the necessary repairs. Nevertheless, if a landline is your only reliable phone option, it may be worth looking into getting this service for setting up your rural home office.

# Internet

Usually, the second largest challenge for working from home in a rural setting is getting adequate Internet service. Fortunately there are several solutions available that can bring the rural home office up to speed. Cellular hotspots and satellite Internet are two of the best solutions, depending on your location.

Many people are surprised at the availability of traditional high speed Internet in the country. If you live in a rural subdivision not too far from town, you may have fiber optic, and cable Internet service. These would probably be about the same speed and capacity as a typical service in the city. Internet has become the focal point for just about everything these days and Internet service providers are reaching ever farther into the countryside in the effort to expand their infrastructure. Unfortunately, many remote rural locations still lag behind, and these services will be unavailable to use. If this is the case at your home, you will have to use alternatives to be able get high speed Internet service.

## *Cellular Hotspots*

These devices use cellular telephone technology to receive Internet connectivity. They receive the signal from a nearby tower and broadcast a home WiFi network that is available for use anywhere inside your home. Most cellular providers have these hotspots available for use with a monthly fee just like a cell phone. Choose from a variety of packages that offer different data limits and speeds to suit your needs. If your cell signal inside your home is too weak, you may still need to use a cellular amplifier inside your home as was discussed previously, to work in conjunction with a cellular hotspot.

The big advantage of using a cellular hotspot is convenience. It automatically configures a home WiFi network with a password of your choice. No other equipment is required and minimal configuring of your WiFi network is necessary. Also these devices are usually very small, and as such they can easily be moved to different rooms inside your house when necessary for better reception.

---

**Handy Tip...**
**When shopping for Cellular WiFi hotspots, look for models that may have external antenna connections. This can greatly increase your success at getting better Internet reliability.**

---

## *Cellular Phone Internet Sharing*

Most modern cell phones have the ability to broadcast an Internet WiFi signal that can be shared with other computers. This can be a really handy option if you need Internet for your laptop while working outside around your property. Another example, is if you loose electricity during a power outage, you can still receive Internet service via sharing a mobile hotpot through your phone. This can be quite useful for checking on updates from the power company's website for information or watching the weather radar for current storm events.

Be aware that using Internet sharing on your phone can quickly burn through your phone's data plan, so keep an eye on your data usage for extended use.

## *Satellite Internet*

Probably the most common way to receive high speed Internet in a very remote rural area is by using satellite Internet services. These services provide a small satellite dish that communicates with various satellites in space. Both inbound and outbound signals are routed through the satellite connection. Much like a satellite television dish, these units are set up permanently and stay focused on the necessary satellite in space at all times. It is usually necessary for the satellite Internet provider to have a professional installer come to your home and set up the equipment.

Most Internet satellite dishes are aimed in a southerly direction. The dish needs a reasonably clear view of the sky in order to work properly. This can present challenges if your home is surrounded by tall trees and no clear southerly view is available. If this is your case you will need to either clear some trees or perhaps use another Internet option. Depending on the necessity of using satellite Internet, you may have to get creative on where you mount your satellite dish in order for it to work properly. In some cases, it may be necessary to mount the satellite dish and it's modem at some distance away from your home. By using network cables buried in the ground, you can route the Internet into your home. The service company's installer can offer many suggestions and help you make the best choice for your particular situation.

Satellite Internet has some advantages and disadvantages. It's biggest advantage is again convenience as once installed, the Internet is always available and ready to use. Many modern satellite modems have built-in routers that will distribute the Internet signals through a dedicated home WiFi network that your devices can connect to. Some providers are expanding their services and launching additional satellites into space yearly, to handle the increased traffic capacity in a lucrative market. Their infrastructure is constantly growing, which is good news for the rural consumer.

Satellite Internet also has some disadvantages. The main disadvantage is that weather can affect the satellite signal and cause temporary interruptions in your Internet service. Rain and heavy fog will sometimes cause a temporary loss of signal. Most signal interruptions only last a short time, usually until the weather clears a bit, and then they will automatically reconnect.

For example, if you are in an important video conference and the weather outside suddenly turns bad, you will be dropped until the rain stops and the signal reconnects. If you use satellite Internet, you will get used to checking the weather before you set up an important Internet task. Heavy rain or thick fog is usually more of a problem, as light rain or mist does not usually affect reception. Additionally, you may have to keep an eye out for any trees or other overgrowth that may block the view of the satellite dish over time. Periodic pruning and clearing of nearby branches and limbs will likely be necessary.

## *Private ISP*

Many rural areas are serviced by private Internet service providers (ISP). These companies set up a regional local network. In most cases, they rent extra space on local radio towers, water towers, and other tall structures to install their antennas. At your home, they also install a smaller antenna and the related equipment that provides Internet. ISP's charge a monthly fee and are usually responsible for maintaining their equipment.

The advantage is that an ISP is a one-stop solution for your Internet needs and they usually offer reliable high-speed data. The disadvantages are that they will typically need a line-of-sight between the antenna at your home to their central antenna located up high on a tower some distance away. If you live in a rural area that is a reasonable distance to town, this is usually not a problem however.

After contacting a private ISP for possible service, they will come to your home and check on their signal strength before setting up any equipment. Lastly, some ISP’s are very small local companies, and some are operated better than others, so it may be wise to ask around with your local neighbors about who they use, and what their overall service is like prior to making a decision on using their services.

## *Building and Construction Considerations*

If you are planning on building a home, you can do a few things in advance during construction that will help improve the cell phone reception inside your home. Metal roofs tend to block many radio signals. They essentially create a shield that prevents weak cell phone signals from penetrating through the metal roof. Using shingles or another non-metalized roofing materials may be an important consideration if inside cell phone reception is vital to you. If your home already has a metal roof, the use of an amplifier and external antenna is recommended.

Many homes are insulated with a metalized foam board in the walls. These too, act like the metal roof in that they can potentially block cell phone signals. Various other types of foam boards are commonly available without the foil coating and these may help prevent signal blockage.

If you are planning a new build, consider carefully designing a wired home network. If you are inexperienced in networking, research the Internet for tips, or better yet, enlist the help of a networking professional to design a system for you. Drawing a schematic of networking cables to your floorplan will aid you considerably in the future. Be sure to include any home theater or entertainment cabling also. While wireless networking is popular, having a wired network within your home generally proves to be faster and more reliable than wireless.

Additionally, make sure to add any networking cables inside the wall framing during construction. Cabling is inexpensive, so consider adding extra cables, more than you think you will need. You'll certainly be glad you did, if needed later on after construction is finished.

# Key Points...

Getting reliable cell phone and Internet coverage can be a challenge for those who live in a rural area. Experimenting with various methods to create a stable and reliable connection, can usually result in suitable connection for most work-from-home situations.

Use a cell phone amplifier with an external antenna to boost cellular reception inside your home.

Consider using a telephone landline if practical for your location.

Cellular hotspot units can be utilized for Internet reception if no other source is available

Satellite Internet is usually the most common method of obtaining high speed Internet in most rural locations.

Many rural locations can receive high speed Internet via a private ISP if your location is not far from town.

When planning to build a new home, take the time to plan a home networking schematic and add extra cabling in the walls during construction for future use.

# Chapter 13

# Seasonal Preparations

One of the most important and necessary tasks for a rural landowner to consider is preparing for the change of seasons. Most homes in the city or suburbia rely on outside utilities, contracted yard maintenance, and municipal maintenance of the streets. As a rural landowner or homeowner, you will likely have to provide these services for yourself. You will want to think ahead and consider what maintenance tasks need to be completed in order to be ready for any potential seasonal weather events.

For example, it is always much easier to winterize your water well system in the nice fall weather versus last minute work in the middle of a winter blizzard. Often these preparations, once completed, will last for several years to come. Regardless, you should think ahead about what your needs will be and make a plan to set aside the necessary time to complete prior to the season change.

# Winter

Winter preparations can vary widely, depending on what part of the country you are located. If you have recently relocated to another state or you are unfamiliar with the upcoming winter weather in your new area, your best information will come from other folks nearby. People living nearby who have already experienced the types of local weather in your area, will be a good source of information. You will likely need to ask around and discuss what preparations will be needed. Additionally, if your property has special considerations, you will need to address those also. For example, if you have water troughs for livestock, you will need to try to prevent those from freezing solid so that your animals have access to fresh water during a blizzard. Usually the winter season will take the most preparation because of the potential for frozen water pipes and protecting your outside animals from the frigid weather.

## *Water Pipes*

The best time to protect your exposed water piping is during the fall months, before the first freeze of the season. Wrapping pipes, covering outside faucets, and winterizing your water well may be your first concern. You can purchase foam pipe insulation at most home centers and hardware stores. These items are usually in short supply during a freeze event, so purchasing them in advance is always a good idea.

Installing foam pipe insulation sleeves is an easy task that requires few tools. The insulation sleeve will already have a split and by using your fingers, you can separate the split and slide the sleeve around a water pipe. Cutting the sleeves to length is easy using either a utility razor knife or ordinary scissors. When wrapping a corner or a joint section, carefully bend the foam sleeve around the corner and try to avoid having any bare areas of piping exposed to the weather. Duct tape can be used to secure the sleeves to form a continuous foam wrap along the pipe sections. Depending on the expected severity of your winter weather, additional protection may be necessary to prevent the pipe from freezing. Electrical heating tape may be necessary for crucial pipes and can be used if an electrical outlet is nearby. For areas that have no electrical outlet, old towels, blankets, and other scrap cloths can be wrapped over the foam insulation to provide additional protection.

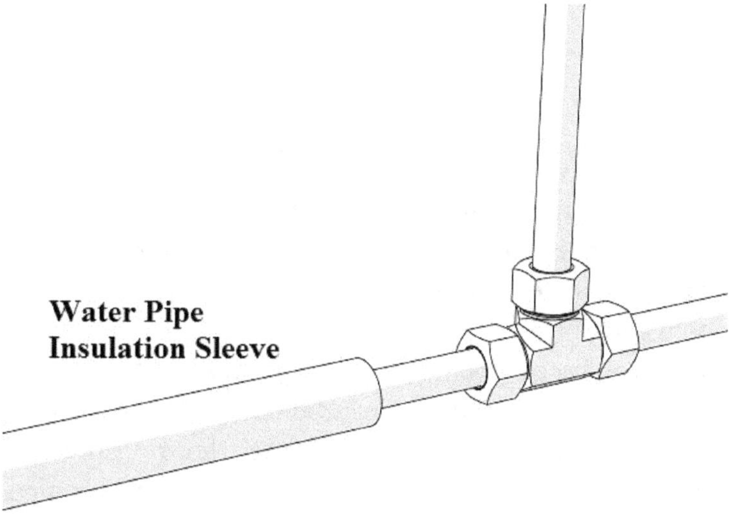


If you live in an area that sustains continual freezes throughout most of the winter, consider installing a frost-proof outdoor faucets. These faucets have the valve located underground below the frost line. They are usually effective for all but the most extreme weather conditions. These can be expensive, and require substantial digging to install. Installing them during the off season warmer months is a good idea, if possible.

You can insulate any exposed water faucets by using the typical hard foam faucet covers that are available at home centers. These covers usually employ an elastic strap that secures the cover over the faucet and the cover provides some freeze protection for the faucet assembly. Again, wrapping the faucet cover with additional scrap towels can be a good idea also.

---

**Handy Tip...**
**Using your water frequently during a hard freeze period is helpful, as it replenishes the water well pressure tank and pipes with naturally warmer water coming from below the surface of the ground. If your well tank and water piping sit static and unused for long periods of time, freezing of the water inside the tank is more likely to occur.**

---

## *Water Wells*

Protecting your well tank from freezing is very important. If your pressure tank freezes solid, it may remain frozen for the remainder of the winter, and you could possibly have no freshwater until the spring thaw. If you live in an area where hard freezes are common, building an insulated well house over your pressure tank is advisable.

By having an enclosed space around your tank, you can then easily keep the space inside the well house above freezing temperatures by using a small electrical heater or heat lamps. If you do not have a well house and your tank is exposed to the weather, using a tank heating blanket is a good solution. These blankets are electrically heated and by wrapping your tank, you can prevent freezing. They do require an electrical outlet. As a precaution, wrap plastic sheeting over the heating blanket to keep it dry from rain or snow.

A good source for non-electrical insulating blankets can be found by utilizing a typical mover's protective blanket. House moving companies use these quilted blankets to protect furniture from scratches when moving. Padded moving blankets can be purchased at most home centers. They tend to be constructed of durable fabric and can be reused each season given proper storage.

As a last resort, if you are expecting a temporary hard freeze event, draining your well tank and piping completely may safely prevent freezing issues, especially if you are unable to be at home. If you utilize this option, remember to shut off all electrical power to your well, to prevent accidental refilling during your absence.

## *Plants and Animals*

Protecting animals should be a primary concern to ensure their welfare during the winter. Valuable plants, shrubs, and flowers should be considered also.

Livestock and other animals need a warm and dry place to protect them from frostbite or freezing to death. A barn or shed will usually suffice, if proper preparations are made ahead of time. Having winter feed in an easily accessible area will be necessary. Making sure to provide some fresh drinking water is very important, as most animals usually drink more often when it is very cold and dry. Keeping livestock such as cows, horses, goats, and sheep can be a huge challenge in the winter, so advance planning is important.

Likewise, protecting important plants such as fruit trees and shrubs can be difficult during a severe winter weather event. Wrapping smaller plants with insulated moving blankets may protect them.

Fruit trees should ordinarily only be planted in areas that rarely experience freezing weather. If a hard freeze is expected, spraying the trees with water may prevent some damage. The ice that will form while spraying can sometimes protect the tender branches and buds from frostbite.

## Keeping Livestock Safe In Winter

**Livestock generally needs more care in the winter months. Most livestock can handle fairly cold temperatures as long as they have these basic needs provided for:**

**1. Adequate feed and hay. Stockpiling feed is a good idea in case of extended blizzards or other storms that may keep you on the property for a good while and you are unable to drive to a feed store.**

**2. Clean fresh water. Water is vitally important, and especially so during a hard freeze. You must remain vigilant and safeguard against freezing water tanks and other vital fresh water sources for animals.**

**3. Shelter. A warm and dry place to shelter during the winter is important for livestock, especially for small or older animals. Warm and dry bedding such as straw or hay will keep them comfortable. Don't forget to provide adequate fresh air if your livestock is inside a closed barn. Dangerous levels of methane gas and carbon dioxide can quickly accumulate and fresh air is important to prevent respiratory ailments in Livestock.**

## *Home Heating*

Firewood is commonly used for both whole house heating and for cozy and decorative fires in the fireplace. If you plan to use firewood, advance preparations will be necessary. The summer season is the best time to cut firewood, as it's usually dry and accessing the forest to cut trees is easier than in the wetter months.

Firewood should be dry and seasoned properly for safety before burning. If you burn freshly cut green wood, dangerous creosote can build up and coat the inside of your chimney. This can be a very dangerous fire hazard and lead to uncontrolled chimney fires.

Wood that is properly dried and seasoned will usually avoid this safety hazard. Exact drying times for different species of hardwood varies with the local weather. Generally, wood that has been dried at least a year under cover from rain, can safely be burned. Again, ask around and get advice from longtime residents in your area. The best type of wood to use, and drying times can be determined from their experience.

Firewood should be protected from the rain and snow. Having some type of shelter is advisable. A simple waterproof tarp placed over the firewood stack can suffice until a more permanent solution is found. Another item to consider is accessibility to your firewood stack. You will be making frequent trips to the woodpile in all types of winter weather, so a suitable and convenient location should be planned in advance. Finally, make sure that you have a sufficient quantity of firewood on hand for the season. Especially so if you use wood as your primary heating source.

If your home uses propane or another source of heat, inspect your heating system carefully before a major winter event. Having your propane storage tank filled well in advance is a good idea. Be sure to turn on your heating system to test for any problems, before winter weather arrives.

## Spring

The spring months usually include storms, rain, and mud. These hazards can make life in the country miserable at times, but planning in advance can help. Spring storms in particular tend to be more intense due to the changing seasonal weather patterns, so taking precautions is prudent. If you live in an area with snow, the melting runoff could cause flooding. Regardless of where you may live, spring mud can be troublesome to deal with.

## *Outdoor Spring Chores*

Re-stain and seal wood decks. Outdoor decks and porches get hammered by winter weather. You can help preserve the life of your wooden decks by sealing them with a deck sealer. Fertilize your lawn after a long winter dormancy. Clean up branches that have fallen from trees, check drainage ditches to make sure they will flow when they need to, especially along side any roads to prevent washout during the heavy spring rains.

## *Storms*

Thunderstorms in the spring can be especially intense. As the atmosphere begins to change from cold to warm, rapid moving cold fronts occur on a steady basis, and these can create intense squall lines. Wind is a particular concern if you live in a rural area. Trees can topple onto power lines and cause power outages that can last for hours or days if severe. It may still be very cold and you will need an alternated source of heat if your home heating relies on electricity for general heating. Having plenty of dry firewood ready to use is a wise idea. Access into or out of your property can be a problem if downed trees cover your entrance road or driveway. Keeping a chainsaw and spare fuel cans ready, should this occur, is always a good idea.

Lightning is a constant danger, especially if you have many tall trees next to your home. As mentioned in an earlier chapter, keeping flammable underbrush cleared away will help protect your home from wildfires.

## *Rain*

Spring is commonly the wettest time of the year for most areas around the country. Flooding from storms or snow melt can turn benign streams into raging torrents quickly.

If this is your first wet spring on your new property, pay particular attention to the natural water drainage and slope of your land. Areas may become underwater that you had not considered, and you may need to figure out a way to re-route heavy water runoff. Also, now is a good time to make sure that any ditches or culverts are clear of debris as they tend to fill throughout the year, and can become ineffective.

### *Mud*

Mud can be very annoying if it impedes your ability to move and work around your property. It's a good idea to keep any potholes that formed over the winter filled, and roads graded to allow for good water drainage. Try to avoid using your tractor unless necessary, as these can quickly create mud bogs and ruts in the soft ground. It's usually a good idea to keep a good pair of high top rubber boots beside the door for convenient use whenever working outside in the mud.

## Summer

After a wet spring, it will feel good to be able to get started on your long list of projects. Summer is the time of the year for working outside. If you live in the southern part of the country, it can get hot and humid quickly, so be aware of getting dehydrated, resulting in dangerous heat exhaustion.

Mowing grass in both your yard and any open pastures will take priority. Make sure to service all of your outdoor equipment such as mowers, tractors, and any other motorized equipment that you may need. Change the oil, charge starting batteries, and tune-ups to lawn equipment will assure their maximum service life.

## Some typical summertime chores may include;

☑ Cutting, splitting, and stacking firewood. As mentioned earlier, it is always best to try to cut firewood far enough ahead so that it can dry and season properly for at least a year before using.

☑ Clearing unwanted overgrowth and other land clearing projects. Since summer is normally dry, this is a good time to tackle projects that require the use of a tractor or other heavy equipment. The dry hard ground means less chances of getting your tractor and other equipment stuck in the mud.

☑ Painting outdoor structures, buildings, and fences. The hot and dry weather will speed drying and hardening of paint.

☑ Yard and landscape projects such as building walkways, sidewalks, and flower beds.

☑ Constructing sheds, outbuildings, or completing any outside building maintenance.

☑ Road and driveway building or maintenance.

Your list may differ, but the dry summer weather will make completing projects much easier, versus working outside in the cold and rain or snow.

## *Vegetable Gardens*

Garden chores can take a large chunk of your time, depending on the size of your vegetable garden. Installing an irrigation system for your garden can relieve you from watering everyday during the heat of the summer. Drip irrigation, or overhead sprinkler systems can be a time saver, otherwise you will find yourself watering your vegetable garden using a water hose morning and evening, nearly everyday.

If you plan on preserving your garden vegetables by canning or freezing, now is the proper time to do that. Vegetables ripen to their peak freshness during the summer months, and that is usually the favored time to harvest them and preserve them for use during the upcoming winter months. Basic canning information can be found in the appendix. If you are fortunate enough to have neighbors nearby who are experienced in preserving vegetables and canning, they can also be a great resource for help and advice.

Towards the end of summer, clean your garden plot of old plants and weeds in preparation for planting a fall garden if desired. Most weeds and grass start to dry up and become dormant during the last part of summer, and thus they can be easier to manage.

If you have compost piles, now is the time to add any additional organic material and turn them for good aeration. Additionally, covering them in preparation for winter rain and snow will help keep them from becoming too wet and saturated.

# Fall

After a hot summer full of work, fall can be considered a pleasant break from most chores. Enjoying the first cool front of the season can be a simple joy to behold. Fall is generally the time to finish up any remaining projects for the year. Giving your yard and property a final cleaning for the year will give you a head start on next year's cycle.

## *Outdoor Fall Chores*

Bring inside and store patio and yard furniture, check gutters and downspouts for clogs or damage, drain and store water hoses.

## *Wildlife*

If you enjoy feeding deer and other wildlife on your property, now is the time to purchase feed and perform maintenance and set up your feeders. Cleaning feeders is important to prevent mold.

While you are out and about on your property, now is also a good time to clean and service any game cameras or security cameras. Replacing batteries, checking memory cards for available space, and moving cameras should be performed while it is still dry.

## *Yards*

Leaves are usually the main cleaning chore for most yards in the fall season. It is important to keep leaves raked and give the soil a chance to breathe and catch the last bits of sunlight for the season. Composting can be very beneficial and fun to do, so now is the time to add all of your leaves and other yard debris into your compost bins.

## *De-Clutter*

Things tend to get a bit cluttered around your property while working in the summer heat. Fall is the time to put away any exposed tools or equipment to protect them from the upcoming winter weather. Other items such as excess building supplies, landscaping materials, and miscellaneous junk tend to accumulate during the summer and weeds will quickly begin to grow around them and create an unsightly mess.

Now is a good time to clean up around your property and properly store your outside materials in a protected location. Bring any tender houseplants inside to protect them from the winter cold and freezing temperatures.

## *Clean Your Heating Source*

If you use wood to heat your home or have a wood burning fireplace, clean it and get it ready for winter use. Be especially careful to clean chimney flues or pipes of any leaves, squirrel nests, loose soot, and creosote buildup. Check smoke detectors, carbon monoxide detectors, and fire extinguishers, and be mindful to replace batteries.

Alternatively, if you use electric heating, clean and service any electric heaters, and don't forget to have your central heating unit coils cleaned before using for the first time this season. Dust tends to collect on heating elements and can catch fire when they are turned on after an extended period of non-use.

## *Stock Up On Livestock Feed And Supplies*

Organize any livestock supplies such as medicine, vaccines, and first aid, and replenish as necessary. This will avoid trying to make an emergency trip to the Veterinarian office during winter snow and ice.

Sacks of livestock feed should be stored in such a manner so that rats and other varmints do not become a problem and contaminate your feed stocks.

Hay for grazing animals should be covered and protected from spoilage by rain and snow.

Your to-do lists may seem long. Your projects keep growing at a faster pace, and keeping up with the seasonal chores can be difficult. Living in the country can sometimes be difficult. It helps to look at the big picture for each season and make a list of chores and projects in their order of importance or urgency. By breaking down your list into smaller chunks, you can generally complete your tasks on time.

Nothing is written in stone, so if you don't get it all done, don't beat yourself up. One of the greatest joys of living in the country is being self sufficient and doing things at your own pace!

# Key Points...

Winter chores should include protecting you water pipes and well system from freeze damage. Give priority to taking care of livestock, pets, and valuable plants and trees. Make sure to have plenty of fresh water available to pets and livestock.
Spring chores should include storm cleanup and road maintenance.
Summer is the time for starting outdoor projects and gardening. Late summer chores include preserving your garden harvest and finishing any uncompleted outdoor projects.
Fall activities should include feeding wildlife, de-cluttering and cleaning your yard and cleaning and maintaining your home heating source in preparation for winter use.

# Chapter 14

# Gardening, Harvest, Food Preservation

One of the many compelling reasons to move from the city to the country is having the ability to grow your own food instead of relying on outside sources. Not only that, but you can grow healthy food that is free of unknown additives. Vegetable gardening can be liberating in the sense that you are in control of your family's diet and you have the ability to make healthy food choices for your family year round.

Beginning gardeners usually should start off with something small and simple by planting in containers and raised beds at first. With more experience, you can eventually plant as large of a garden as your property allows. Everyone's soil and climate is a bit different, so it takes some time and experimentation to find out what works successfully for your family's individual needs.

## Types of Gardens

The term garden has many connotations and meanings depending on your geographic locale. For the purpose of this chapter, a garden is a plot that produces food such as vegetables and fruits. To narrow it down a bit more, there are several types and sizes of vegetable gardens and fruit orchards.

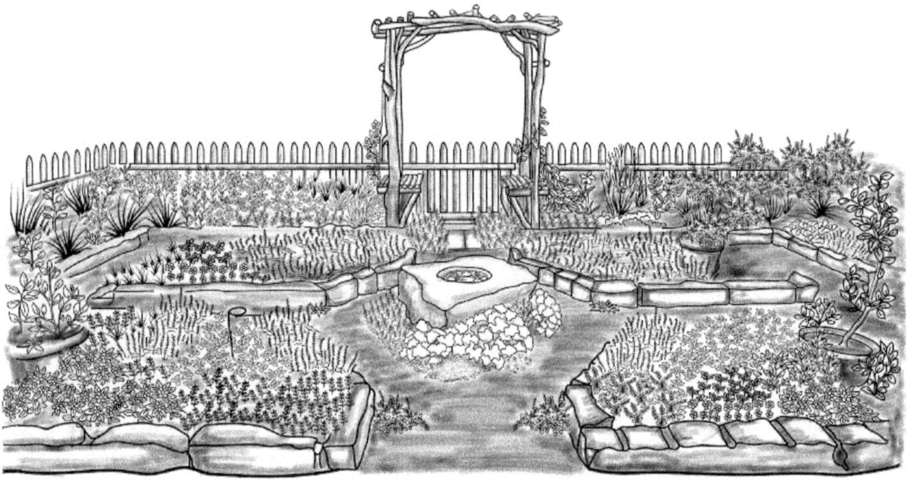

## *Kitchen Gardens*

A kitchen garden is an old concept that came into use many generations ago. It was a very small garden that was located just outside of the kitchen area of a home. This garden was usually separate from any other larger vegetable garden plots and was used mainly to grow herbs and other aromatics for use in cooking. Since it was located just steps away from the food prep area in the kitchen, it was easily available and convenient. The cook would just step outside and grab a handful of selected herbs and quickly wash and cook them.

A kitchen garden is still a wonderfully convenient asset to any rural property, even today. One can also incorporate small greenhouses, potting areas, and even water features into our kitchen gardens to make them even more versatile and beautiful at the same time. If your rural property is small, a kitchen garden may be all that you can manage. Likewise, if your household is small, a small kitchen garden may be all the garden that you really need.

There are really no set rules in what should be grown in a typical kitchen garden. Edible and medicinal herbs are always a staple in any kitchen garden and just about any vegetable can be incorporated as long as it is a reasonably small plant. For example, plants that tend to produce very long runners such as watermelons and cantaloupes would probably be better managed in a full sized garden, instead of taking over the small space of a kitchen garden.

Vegetables such as tomatoes, beans, and potatoes would be a perfect size along with leafy greens for fresh salads. Any vegetable or herb that tends to be high priced in stores when compared to growing them yourself would be an excellent choice as long as they have a relatively small footprint.

## *Vegetable Gardens*

A full sized vegetable garden can take on many forms - such as a traditional row crop garden or a raised bed garden. Both types have advantages and disadvantages. A row-crop garden can cover many acres of land if desired, and can produce enormous amounts of vegetables. Most market or commercial gardens are row-crop style because a tractor and various implements can be used for tillage, planting, and harvesting of the vegetables. Even a small row-crop garden can be managed with a small tractor. Irrigation can be incorporated such as overhead sprinkler systems or drip style irrigation using drip tape along the rows.

The disadvantages of a row-crop garden are weed control and pest and animal control. Weeds can quickly outrun any vegetables in a row-crop garden and pests and animals such as rabbits and deer can be a real problem.

Raised bed gardening has become more popular in recent years. The biggest advantages of a raised bed garden are weed control and soil management are easier. Due to the fact that a raised bed is a contained area, weeds are easily managed and removed versus a traditional row-crop garden at ground level. Small animals such as rabbits and gophers are usually not a problem in high raised beds. You can also fill a raised bed with any soil mixture that you want, regardless of your native soil conditions on your property. Lastly, a tall raised bed is very convenient for older folks and others who have difficulty bending over.

The disadvantages of a raised bed garden are mainly logistical. Raised beds can be expensive to build and maintain. Pathways and walkways between the beds are necessary and require occasional weeding or mowing. The soil in raised beds tends to dry out easily and as a result, more frequent watering is necessary when compared to a row-crop garden.

One last type of vegetable garden deserves mention. These gardens are really just vegetables grown in containers such as pots, buckets, bags, etc. Most first-time gardeners usually start by growing their first vegetables in containers. Even folks in urban areas can utilize a container garden if they have no other space available. In a rural setting, a container garden can be really useful for growing vegetables the first year that you are on your property. You may not know what the weather in your new area will bring, and what plants grow well. Rainfall patterns and sunlight throughout the year need to be studied and determined before a permanent garden area can be built. By utilizing vegetables grown in movable containers such as buckets or pots, you can still enjoy gardening while determining where to build a suitable long-term garden plot.

## *Fruit Orchards*

If you desire to grow fruit trees, several considerations must be met in order to be successful for the long term. The local prevailing climate is a prime concern for many fruit tree varieties. Since many varieties of fruit can be damaged by cold and frost, you should research what will actually grow in your area. Talk with local residents and visit with your local co-op representative to get information. Sunlight plays an important role for fruit tree growth and having the necessary means to water your trees during periods of drought should also be considered. Your soil may need to be amended and conditioned as necessary so that your fruit trees can get the necessary nutrients to produce successfully.

Because of the slow growing nature of fruit trees, a fruit orchard should be considered a long-term investment in your property. It may be several years before you are able to harvest any fruit and realize any benefits from your hard work. When compared to the relatively quick production of vegetables, fruit trees take much more effort and patience.

# Garden Planning

## *Sizing a Garden*

One mistake often made by rural newcomers is planting an over sized garden. Since you now have the extra space, it's very tempting to jump in head first and plant a huge row-crop garden with many types of vegetables. What usually happens next is that weeds tend to take over and make a mess, and watering becomes difficult because it was not well thought out when first planting. Some plants burn up in the hot sunlight while others tend to grow small and stunted with too much shade. All of this is the result of poor or no planning.

When planning a garden area, be specific about your expectations. Are you just wanting a bit of fresh vegetables for your family, or do you want to sell large quantities at a farmer's market?

The majority of city folks moving to a rural area, have little experience in gardening and will be better served by growing a small garden initially, until they get more experience. Even a small container garden or a kitchen garden may be all that is needed, and these types of gardens are much more manageable.

## *Realistic Expectations*

The reality of gardening is that no spot is perfect and some difficulties will be encountered. Problems such as pests, disease, wrong amounts of sunlight, nutrients, and water, can make a garden labor intensive and expensive to manage. Wild animals such as deer, rabbits, and wild hogs can destroy a garden area overnight. Sometimes it seems that gardening is just about impossible. Having a realistic view that gardening will not always be easy or successful from year to year is important. When you encounter problems, try to work out a way to manage them and try not to get discouraged as it eventually happens to every gardener.

## *Garden Logistics*

All vegetables need sunlight, water, and nutrients from the soil in order to grow well and produce healthy vegetables. These three things are paramount to success. Locating and designing your garden area should take all these into account.

Sunlight is probably the most important factor when designing a garden area. Most vegetables need full sun in order to thrive. Depending on your location, you may get more hours of direct sun when compared to a garden located in northern regions of the country.

Not all plants can tolerate direct heat and sunlight, so research what grows well in your region and plant accordingly. Avoid placing your garden area directly under large trees. You want to orient garden's position so that the plants get the maximum amount of sunlight as the sun passes overhead throughout the day.

Water is the next major consideration when planning a garden. As discussed earlier in this book, your rural property should have a water well or perhaps municipal water is available. Additionally, you may need to install a permanent water faucet connection near your garden if one is not already available. This will allow you to attach a water hose or install an irrigation system to provide water to your garden during times of drought.

Soil type and composition is important for garden success. One of the very first things you should do is get a professional soil test done for the direct area of your garden. These are usually done by digging small samples of the native soil from your prospective garden plot and sending them to a professional soil test laboratory for analysis. These tests will tell you what nutrients are missing from your soil and usually how much to add for the types of vegetables that you intend to grow. Again, your local co-op agent is invaluable in helping you with these tests when necessary. It's usually possible to get whatever soil amendments that are necessary delivered to your garden area by your local landscape suppliers.

## Harvesting

## *Harvesting and Preserving Basics*

You may be pleasantly surprised to find out that your small garden produces more vegetables than you expected. You will need to be prepared to harvest your vegetables throughout the growing season as most vegetables rarely ripen for harvest all at once.

By using modern methods, such as freezing, combined with traditional methods of preservation, such as canning, you can happily harvest and save your vegetables all season long with little waste.

## *Freezing*

Modern kitchens have freezers included in their design, and fortunately most garden vegetables can be frozen while retaining their nutrients and freshness. The advantage of freezing fresh vegetables is that you can easily freeze small quantities as the vegetables ripen and you can keep adding more vegetables with very little waste. It's easy, quick, and efficient. The disadvantages are that not all vegetables freeze well due to their water content, and some vegetables will loose their flavor slightly after freezing. For example; melons such as water melons do not freeze well because of their high water content. Also keep in mind that a freezer is wholly dependent on electricity, and periods of extended power outages can spoil an entire season's harvest all at once.

---

**Handy Tip...**
**Rural kitchens may benefit from the addition of extra freezer space, especially if gardening is a goal. Consider adding an additional freezer into your kitchen or pantry design.**

---

## *Canning*

The term canning is a bit of a misnomer these days as it nearly always refers to preserving food in glass jars and not metal cans. Canning is a method of preserving various vegetables and meats in a liquid inside glass jars that are sealed in a vacuum under high heat and pressure. This allows food to be safely preserved, and free of deadly bacteria and germs.

Once the jars are sealed properly, they can be stored long term on a shelf without any electricity or outside assistance. Most canned vegetables can be safely stored for several years under suitable conditions, and once they are opened, the vegetables inside are as fresh and delicious as when they were first harvested.

Canning can be very useful when you suddenly have a large amount of a single vegetable type. For example; if you have a bushel of ripe tomatoes, you can process them into a large batch of homemade tomato sauce and by canning, you can store your sauce for easy consumption when desired throughout the year. You may also can to preserve vegetable combinations such as potatoes and green beans or okra and tomatoes together to create tasty and convenient all-in-one side dishes.

Canning is not difficult, but it must be done in a precise and exacting manner in order to be safe. Absolutely no short cuts are allowed in the canning process. The USDA has perfected and published canning directions for many years. These guidelines to safe canning are very specific in their directions. Item specifics such as processing time, pressures, and methods should be followed exactly to ensure that the jars are sealed properly and the food inside is free of bacteria and germs. If in doubt about a particular canning process, always refer to the USDA preservation instructions. More information can be found in the appendix of this book and the USDA website. Additionally, many canning jar manufacturing companies have published their own books and guides for the home canning process.

## *Drying and Dehydrating*

Many vegetables can be dried and preserved safely as long as the moisture is removed and the dried food is stored properly. Drying and dehydrating are very closely related. Both produce the same results using different methods. Which method to use is normally determined by the size and shape of the vegetable. For example, herbs can be easily placed inside an electric dehydrator and processed in just a day or two. On the other hand, a large batch of full sized onions will need to be hung up with string or placed on drying racks outside. This make take several weeks when drying naturally.

Electric dehydrators are cheap to purchase and very easy to use. Basically they are very low temperature drying ovens. Usually small metal or plastic racks are stacked vertically over a small heating element. Warm air is slowly rises up and around the vegetables and expelled out the top of the dehydrator. This method greatly accelerates the drying process and can do a good job of preserving vegetables like herbs, beans, carrots, etc. Once the food is sufficiently dried, it is good practice to store them  in airtight freezer bags or inside dry and sealed canning jars. To use dried vegetables, you simply re-hydrate them in a bit of boiling water on the stove.

## Food Pantries

# *Food Pantry Design Basics*

After you have a large batch of nicely preserved vegetables from your garden, you will likely want a place to store them for use throughout the year.

Having a large food pantry is a country tradition that has it's roots coming from the Depression era when folks realized that stocking up on food was both important and necessary. Recently, food pantries are making a popular comeback for many of the same reasons. Food shortages have unfortunately become commonplace again, and having a well stocked food pantry helps buffer the uncertainties in our food supply chain.

Additionally, a large food pantry can help with absorbing dramatic price fluctuations that go hand in hand with food shortages. Buying items in bulk when they are easily available and on sale, will keep you from needing to purchase the same items when they are in short supply and expensive.

If you have the available space, a walk-in style of pantry is ideal for most families. Having a row of shelves for food items allows for easy management and restocking as you can easily see what items are low and how much you already have on hand. Additionally, you can sort and organize food items into groups such as canned goods, packaged food, dry goods, and so forth. If possible, it is very convenient to have ample counter space to store various cooking accessories that tend to take up valuable counter space in the kitchen. Items such as mixers, microwaves, air fryers, and other occasionally used cooking appliances are still available for quick use, yet out of the way while you are preparing a meal in the kitchen. If you are designing a walk-in style of food pantry from scratch, be sure to include ample electrical outlets for these items.

If you need a place to store all of your preserved foods, such as from your canning activities during the summer, a cool and dark place is ideal for long term storage. Try to avoid storing preserved food in harsh sunlight as the UV rays will cause the natural color of canned vegetables to bleach out quickly.

If your current situation only allows for a smaller cabinet or closet style of food pantry, then consider using plastic shelf organizers to maximize the use of the space that is available. Larger bulk food items such as pet food bags can be stored in another accessible location or utility closet nearby.

If you store long-term food items in your basement, moisture and insects need to be carefully controlled. Sealing dried food in vacuum seal bags is an excellent way of keeping contaminants outside and freshness inside. Additionally, plastic buckets or pails with good, airtight sealing lids will allow for storing large quantities of food in a small space.

Always use clean food grade buckets. These can be easily sourced new online or purchased used and reasonably priced from restaurants and shops such as donut shops, etc.

Whatever food storage designs that you use, it is important to label your food packages with a purchase date and rotate your food stock so that the oldest items are consumed first. Keep a vigilant eye for insects, ants, and other problems. Lastly, it is always helpful to keep an on-going shopping list of foods that are running low, in a visible place near the pantry to help make grocery shopping more efficient.

# Key Points

Pick the type and style of garden that most suits your personal needs. Make sure that you keep realistic expectations when confronted with gardening problems.

When designing a garden area, make sure to accommodate the three key necessities for successful plant growth - sunlight, water, and soil nutrients. A professional laboratory soil test is crucial for determining your present soil condition and what amendments are needed, and how much to apply for the vegetables that you intend to grow.

Harvesting is an important part of gardening and food preservation needs to be convenient, and done properly for food safety. Freezing, canning, and drying of vegetables are the most commonly used methods of food preservation.

Storing preserved food is an important step, and having a food pantry that allows for bulk storage is a good idea. By using bulk storage methods, food can be stockpiled when readily available, to avoid shortages and large price fluctuations.

# Chapter 15

# Dealing With the Unexpected

Living in a rural area can often times mean dealing with unexpected problems. Being self-reliant also means being responsible for coping with unexpected problems that may crop up at the worst times. On the other hand, being prepared for these problems will give you the confidence to face these challenges. In cities, emergencies are often handled by municipal services or neighborhoods and neighbors are more plentiful than in your new rural homestead location now. With your ability to be prepared , you will just face the issues at hand and work out the necessary solutions for yourself.

## *Illness*

Everyone gets sick occasionally and if you live in the country, this can have cascading problems that may be unforeseen. For example, if you get the flu and are bedridden for a few weeks, your property will still be needing daily care regardless of how you may feel. Grass will need to be mowed, animals cared for, and so goes the list… If you neglect these tasks while you are sick, bad things can quickly multiply and become significant issues.

Having a well stocked medicine kit is a must for rural living. Doctors and medical care may not be readily available, and you need to have a means of self medication and care during times of minor illness. Take the time to stock up on first aid supplies such as bandages, wound-care supplies, and have a sufficient supply of over-the-counter medicine to handle any mishaps or minor illness. A good idea for storing first aid supplies and extra medicine is to use a plastic storage bin or perhaps a typical plastic cabinet with several drawers. If you cut yourself badly, you need to be able to easily locate the proper first-aid supplies with little effort. Over-the counter drugs for ailments such as diarrhea, colds, flu, and typical minor illnesses need to be stocked ahead of time. Remember the pharmacy is not just around the corner. Having these supplies readily at hand is crucial.

If you become too ill to take care of your daily duties and chores, make sure that any other family members can at least keep the household running smoothly. For example, being the only one in the family that knows how to feed your livestock is setting yourself up for major problems if you are unable to do it yourself. Likewise, make sure that other family members know where to access any tools, equipment, or other supplies that may be needed.

## *Pet Emergencies*

Your pets can be exposed to more dangers when you live in the country. Another often unrealized problem are fleas, ticks, and other parasites. These problems can get out of hand quickly for animals that live in a rural area. Also, keeping your pets safe from wild animals, snakes, and other dangers requires much more diligence than living in the city. Pre-treat your pets with flea prevention medicine and make sure that they have the proper rabies vaccines and shots. Take the time to know where your closest veterinarian is located for serious problems. Ask your neighbors where they get their animals treated. Be aware that rural veterinarians sometimes specialize in treating large animals such as livestock versus household pets. It would be wise to research in advance of purchasing livestock (or additional animals), the options for veterinary care that you may have available in your local area. Be sure that you know in advance if your veterinarian can treat whatever pets or livestock you may have.

## *Property Damage*

Weather can be unpredictable regardless of location, but storms often have considerably more impacts to rural property when compared to city lots. Trees can topple onto roads or fences. Flooding may be a problem on your property. Livestock may get loose if a fence gets damaged. As mentioned earlier, having a good working chainsaw and extra fuel on hand can be a true necessity. One of the benefits of rural living is having the extra space to stock up and store emergency supplies. Items such as fence building supplies, spare lumber, and extra road building materials, will assure that you can quickly repair most major problems that may occur.

These days, small generators are commonly available. Having a small and portable generator is not only handy for daily use in remote areas of your property, it can also be a real help in a power outage to help keep refrigerators and freezers cold.

Knowing how to properly use a small generator for emergency power around your home is very important and requires pre-planning to assure your safety.

---

**Handy Tip...**
**Tarps can have many uses on a rural property. Having an assortment of heavy duty tarps in several sizes can be very useful for quickly weatherproofing roofs, walls, or animal enclosures, until a permanent repair can be done.**

---

## *Stray Animals*

One of the bittersweet aspects of living in the country is that stray animals will sometimes suddenly appear at your door. Knowing how to safely and properly deal with these situations is sometimes important. Depending on the animal, it is always important to keep safety for your family and pets in mind. If a large and dangerous animal such as a bear, feral hog, or deer gets into your yard, keep your children and pets inside. If necessary, call your local game warden. They will have the proper knowledge to handle a dangerous animal. Other smaller wild animals such as raccoons, foxes, and birds should most often be left alone. Wild animals by nature, can usually take care of themselves. Avoid leaving food, and other things that may attract curious or hungry wild animals.

Sadly, many times dogs and cats will show up. It can be tempting to feed them and hope that they go away. Unfortunately that's not usually the case, and as such, you need to be selective on any stray dogs or cats that you wish to keep. We all love animals, but sometimes you must make a decision on which animals you choose to make pets.

## *Extended Absences*

Occasionally, you may need to take an extended absence from your property. You may want to take a vacation trip, visit relatives, or work a temporary job someplace distant. Whatever the reason, your property will remain behind and someone will need to look after it. You should make arrangements in advance for a helper to take care of your animals, look after your property, and for security. Before you leave, plan ahead if possible, and take the time to familiarize your helper with the steps needed to properly take care of whatever ongoing chores that will needed to continue in your absence.

Unlike your city counterparts who can just leave home freely with minimal preparation when desired, a rural property has many more responsibilities and as such, you need to make sure that you have someone to step in and properly maintain things around your property in your absence.

# Key Points...

The key to dealing with unexpected problems is advance preparation. Have a plan in place, in case a weather disaster strikes, you get sick, or if a dangerous animal shows up in your yard.

Keeping spare supplies, a good first aid kit, and extra help, can make dealing with unexpected problems easier.

Take the time to locate a local veterinarian and make sure that they can treat all of your animals when necessary.

When taking an extended absence, make sure to have a helper to look after your property and make sure that they know where to find things around your property when needed.

# Appendix

## Warm and cool season grass characteristics:

| WARM SEASON GRASSES | Cold Tolerant | Heat Tolerant | Drought Tolerant | Shade Tolerant |
|---|---|---|---|---|
| St. Augustine grass | | X | | X |
| Bermuda grass | X | X | X | |
| Zoysia grass | X | X | | X |
| Bahia grass | | X | | X |
| Buffalo grass | X | X | X | |

| COOL SEASON GRASSES | | | | |
|---|---|---|---|---|
| Kentucky Bluegrass | X | X | X | |
| Creeping Bentgrass | X | X | | X |
| Colonial Bentgrass | X | | | X |
| Tall Fescue | | X | X | X |
| Fine Fescue | X | | X | X |

## Cool season grass, warm season grass, and transitional zone map:

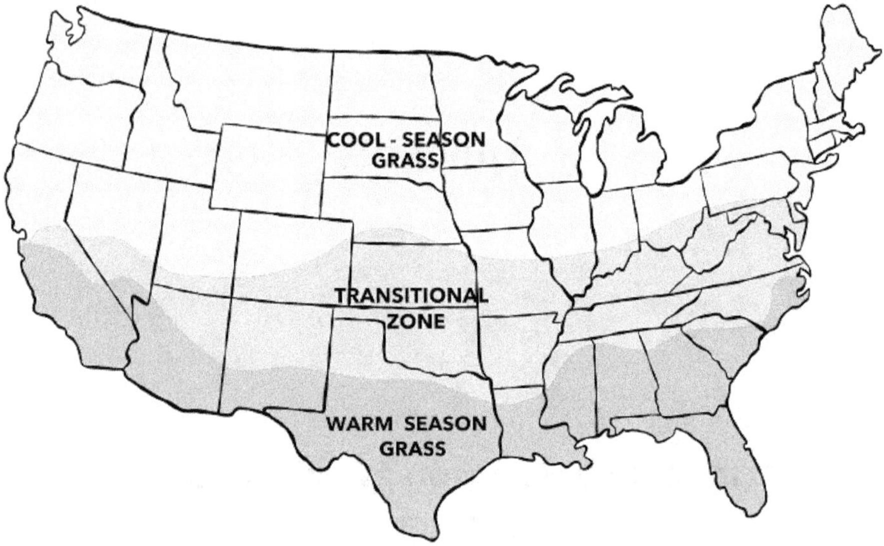


---

| Annual Herbs | Perennial Herbs |
|---|---|
| Basil | Beebalm |
| Calendula | Chives |
| Cilantro | Fennel |
| Dill | Lavender |
| Parsley | Lemon Balm |
| | Marjoram |
| | Mint |
| | Oregano |
| | Rosemary |
| | Sage |
| | Tarragon |
| | Thyme |

## Best times to water:

**Lawns** - Water deeply but infrequently. Wait until the turf shows signs of distress. This promotes healthy root development deep into the soil. Water early in the day if possible so that the water has time to evaporate off of the leaves before nightfall to discourage fungal disease.

**Flowers and Vegetables** - For shallow rooted plants and flowers such as most annuals, water every day in hot weather. Plants in containers or pots dry out quickly and may need daily watering. If a plant shows signs of stress and the soil is dry, water daily and add mulch if possible around the roots to help preserve moisture between waterings. Vegetable gardens planted directly in the ground will need water every few days. During times of drought, daily watering may be needed. Watering in the morning is preferred, except if bees are pollinating the flowers, then late afternoon watering is acceptable. Avoid spraying water on plants during the hottest part of the day with direct sunlight, as scalding can occur. Avoid watering after dark to discourage fungal growth and diseases.

**Trees and Shrubs** - Water newly planted trees every other day to encourage root growth. For large and established trees, use a drip hose in the area under and the same diameter as the tree canopy. Water deeply to allow water to penetrate at least 12 inches into the soil if possible. Overnight watering may be needed during times of drought. Mulching smaller trees can preserve moisture for shallow roots.

## Soil PH Chart

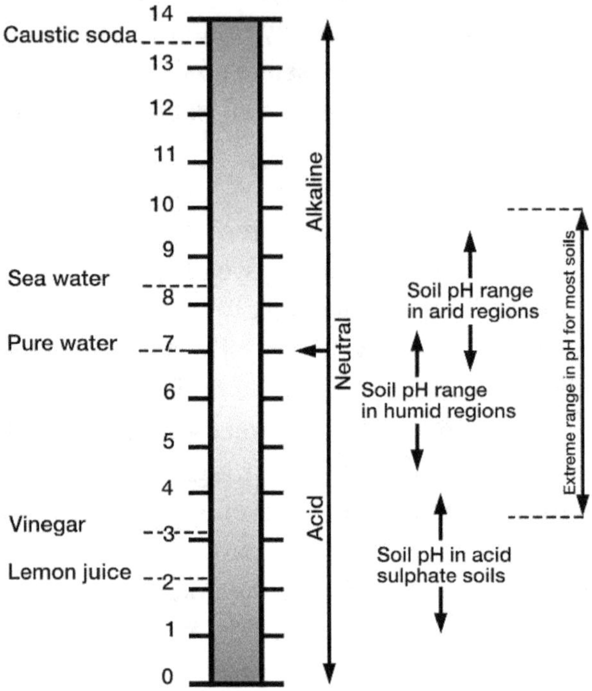


| | |
|---|---|
| 4.9 or below | add 20 lbs. of lime per 100 sq.ft. Incorporate well into new garden bed or make 4 applications of 5 lbs. each to established gardens. |
| 5.0 - 5.5 | add 10 lbs. of lime per 100 sq. ft. Mix half in and rake the other half into the surface of a new garden. |
| 5.6 - 6.4 | add 5 lbs. of lime per 100 sq. ft. |
| 6.5 - 7.4 | no lime needed. |
| 7.5 - 7.9 | add 1 lb. sulfur per 100 sq. ft. |
| 8.0 - 8.9 | add 2 lbs. sulfur per 100 sq. ft. |

## Common flower planting and blooming:

| Flower | Plant Type | Planting Season | Blooming Season |
|---|---|---|---|
| Amaranth | AN | SPR | SPR-SUM |
| Aster | PER | SPR | SPR-SUM-F |
| Begonia | PER | SPR | SPR-SUM |
| Black-eyed Susan | AN PER | SPR | SUM-F |
| Canna | BULB | SPR | SUM-F |
| Cape Marigold | AN | SPR | SUM |
| Columbine | PER | F or SPR | SPR-SUM |
| Cosmos | AN | SPR | SUM-F |
| Impatiens | AN | SPR | SUM |
| Iris | PER | F | SPR-SUM |
| Lantana | PER | SPR | SPR-SUM-F |
| Marigold | AN | SPR | SUM-F |
| Primrose | AN PER | SPR | W-SPR |
| Sage | AN PER | SPR | SUM |
| Sunflower | AN | SPR | SUM-F |

## Common Trees and Bushes For Wildlife:

| Tree | Part of tree | Wildlife it attracts |
|---|---|---|
| American Beech | Nuts<br>Leaves | Squirrels, Butterflies |
| Buckeye | Flowers | Hummingbirds |
| Butterfly bush | Flowers | Butterflies, Bees |
| Desert Willow | Flowers | Hummingbirds |
| Dogwood | Berries | Squirrels, Birds |
| Hawthorn | Berries<br>Shelter | Birds |
| Hickory | Nuts<br>Bark | Squirrels.<br>Woodpeckers |
| Holly | Berries<br>Shelter | Birds |
| Juniper | Berries | Birds |
| Lilac | Flowers<br>Leaves<br>Shelter | Butterflies, Bees,<br>Deer, Birds |
| Maple | Seeds | Squirrels |
| Oak | Acorn | Birds, Squirrels, Deer |
| Birch | Leaves | Birds, Butterflies |
| Pine | Cones<br>Twigs<br>Shelter | Squirrels, Birds,<br>Browsing game |

## When To Prune Trees and Shrubs:

| Plant | When to Prune | Why |
|---|---|---|
| Arborvitae | after spring bloom | shape growth |
| Azalea | after spring bloom | shape growth |
| Boxwood | late winter | shape as hedge |
| Butterfly Bush | early spring | cut back old growth to start new wood |
| Daphne | after flowering | shape growth |
| Forsythia | after spring bloom | shape for hedge, cut back old growth to start new wood |
| Holly | winter, early spring | cuttings for seasonal decoration |
| Juniper | late winter | shape as hedge |
| Lilac | after spring bloom | remove suckers, deadhead, shape for growth |
| Mock Orange | after spring bloom | keep overgrowth in check |
| Mountain Laurel | after spring bloom | keep overgrowth in check |
| Nandina | early spring, summer | shape growth, remove berries |
| Pine | late spring, summer | clip top candle for size |
| Rhododendron | after spring bloom | shape growth |

## USDA Food Canning and Preservation Online Links and Information

**National Center for Home Food Preservation:**
nchfp.uga.edu

**Principles of Home Canning:**
https://nchfp.uga.edu/publications/usda/GUIDE01_HomeCan_rev0715.pdf

**Selecting, Preparing, and Canning Fruit and Fruit Products:**
https://nchfp.uga.edu/publications/usda/GUIDE02_HomeCan_rev0715.pdf

**Selecting, Preparing, and Canning Vegetables and vegetable Products:**
https://nchfp.uga.edu/publications/usda/GUIDE04_HomeCan_rev0715.pdf

**Preparing and Canning Jams and Jellies:**
https://nchfp.uga.edu/publications/usda/GUIDE07_HomeCan_rev0715.pdf

# Basic Food Pantry Staple List

**Milk & Dairy**
Milk & Cream
Yogurt
Cheese
Cottage Cheese
Cream Cheese
Eggs
Butter
Margarine
Sour Cream
Ice Cream

**Fruit & Vegetable**
Apples
Bananas
Oranges
Grapes
Pears
Tomatoes
Lettuce
Spinach
Kale
Squash
Potatoes
Onions
Scallions
Garlic
Peppers
Cucumbers
Carrots
Celery
Mushrooms

**Frozen Foods**
Juices
Vegetables
- Asparagus
- Corn
- Mixed
- Peas (Carrots)
- Fries (Tots)

Fruit
- Strawberries
- Blueberries
- Blackberries
- Raspberries

**Canned & Dry Goods**
Green Beans
Corn
Tomato Sauce
Soups
Pasta
- Spaghetti
- Fettuccine
- Lasagna
- Elbow Macaroni

Rice
Dried Beans
- Pinto
- Navy
- Black
- Kidney
- Lima

Crackers
Salad Dressing
Mayonnaise
Ketchup
BBQ Sauce
Relish/Pickles
Olives
Salsa
Worcestershire Sauce
Cereal
- Cold Cereals
- Oatmeal

Honey
Assorted Chips

**Baking Products**
Flour
Corn Meal
Sugar/Powdered Sugar
Brown Sugar
Baking Chocolate
Raisins
Nuts
Non-Stick Cooking Spray
Peanut Butter
Vinegar
Shortening
Spices
Baking Soda
Baking Powder
Vanilla Flavoring
Cake Mixes
Frostings
Evaporated Milk
Coconut

**Meats**
Roast Beef
Ground Beef
Ground Turkey
Pork Chops
Sausage
Ham
Chicken
Wieners
Bacon
Steaks

**Bread Products**
Bread White
Bread Whole Wheat
Buns
Tortillas

**Paper Products**
Paper Towels
Napkins
Waxed Paper
Aluminum Foil
Plastic Storage Bags
Toilet Tissue

**Miscellaneous**
Coffee
Coffee Filters
Hot Chocolate
Sodas

**Pet Supplies**
Cat Food
Dog Food
Treats
Cat Litter

# INDEX

Note: Page numbers in *italic* indicate illustrations; those in **boldface** indicate charts or tables.

# Y

www.ingramcontent.com/pod-product-compliance
Lightning Source LLC
LaVergne TN
LVHW051828080426
835512LV00018B/2782

* 9 7 9 8 2 1 8 3 3 5 3 0 4 *